Sheri Dixon

Aln
A Different Kind of Survival Story

By Sheri Dixon

**Copyright 2009 by Sheri Dixon.
The author retains sole copyright to her contributions to this book.**

ISBN-13: 978-0615679020

I dedicate this book to

The Human Race

Get Well Soon

You had such potential…

Prologue

Can we turn on the television or read the news without being bombarded with proof of our imminent demise from some huge disaster?

Peak oil, terrorism from within and without our borders, Swine Flu, Bird Flu, pollution of our minds and our bodies, SOMEthing SOMEone SOMEwhere is going to be our un-doing.

People are running scared, running on empty, running towards salvation and away from danger- only which is which is sometimes difficult to tell.

Stoking and stroking it all are books, manuals, movies, docu-dramas and reality shows instructing the human race on the best ways to protect itself from itself.

Stop.
Listen.

The really important things
Are often
Almost Invisible.

Recipe for Being Human

Water

Food

Shelter

Security

Health

Community

Faith

Combine all ingredients
Stir gently
Extremely perishable
Yet amazingly resilient

**Chapter Zero
Our Heroine**

In the beginning, it troubled her to be almost invisible.

She was a little annoyed when other people were noticed, listened to, acknowledged- their existence confirmed and affirmed by the reflection of others' responses to them.

"May I help you?" the clerk asked the man behind her in line.

"Nice day, isn't it?" the woman sitting between her and the window on the bus smiled to the woman across the aisle.

Children saw her. They always smiled and waved at her.

And dogs. Dogs always liked her.

Cats? Well, it's difficult to tell with cats.

But by and large, she was just not there for the entire adult population of the human race.

After a while, she got used to it and stopped caring.

Part One

2008

"Stir Gently"

<u>Chapter One</u>

<u>Water</u>

She didn't stop caring in a depressed or angry way. She just had other things to do.

She'd been looking for a place for a long time- she couldn't exactly put a finger on just how long, but knew it was about 40 years, give or take. 'Course, she didn't rightly know how old she really was either, damn those memory lapses anyway.

The medication wasn't effective. It just cost money and made her fuzzy so she stopped taking it.

Then her doctor fussed at her and said, "I can't help you if you won't take your medicine".

So she stopped going to the doctor.

Seemed the sensible thing to do.

Anyway, the place.

Although she'd been looking for years, it wasn't an active organized look-in-the-classifieds sort of search.

More of an "I'll keep my eyes open and know it when I see it" sort of search.

The One True Thing she knew about this place was that it had water. Salt water, running water, standing water, murky turgid frog-infested water- she wasn't exactly for sure what KIND of water, but water there would be.

Had to be, her brain told her.

For some reason, just out of reach in her memory.

Just seemed right, so it was.

That year it seemed that water was everywhere in the news.

There was a hurricane down on the Gulf, again.

Big one.

Washed away a lot of civilization.

Left nothing but a beach, or what would be a beach once the clean up crews toted away all the crumpled remains of peoples' lives, and a lot of the remains of the people themselves.

'Course, she had no TV. All this she learned from the families at the shelter. The New People- coming in burdened with small children and large sadness, no money, no possessions, but a lot of worry, and a never-ending supply of hopelessness.

These children didn't smile at her.

Their pinched little faces were clouded with the loss of everything they'd known. They stared at offerings of treats or small toys with distrust and hesitated to take them. Once in their hands, though, these same items became treasures.

She couldn't abide the mass of emptiness, so she spent much of her time walking, sitting in the park, smiling at children who still had homes and toys and pets- children who could still smile back.

One afternoon, she picked up a newspaper that was left on the bench beside her when its owner finished with it and walked off- he'd never said a word to her or even looked in her direction- just sat down, caught up with world events or sports or the latest political bru ha ha, and once he felt connected to the world again, he got up and walked away.

If someone had asked him to describe her five minutes later, he would've looked mildly surprised and asked, "There was someone there? Huh. Weird".

But it wouldn't have bothered him.

Tucked into the center pages of the paper- after the national news, after the local news, but before the editorials and obituaries, was a group of small articles about the drought.

She read them with interest, wondering at the oddness of half of a huge state being dragged by swirling walls of rain into the sea while the other half parched and blew away.

And she thought of the people, the families, who lost everything because of water- or the lack thereof.

It was Wednesday.

Wednesday was sprinkler day at the park, and she always tried to be there to watch the children playing in the fountains.

But the sprinklers didn't turn on. There were no children splashing like little rainbow fishes in the glittering diamond waterspouts.
Instead, there was a note.

It was typed. And looked very official.

Due to the current water shortage
There will be no watering of gardens or lawns
allowed
Until further notice.

Well, this was disappointing.

Others were disappointed as well.

The children and their mothers sighed and went on to something different to do with their mornings- beach towels trailing behind them like so many wilted flowers.

On the far side of the dormant fountains is a historical marker- not a statue or monument- just a tiny dark metal sign stating that this park sits on the site of the very first homestead in the county- the family's name given to the park though the family had long since died or moved on and their farm, their home, had gone first idle, then into disrepair, then quietly fallen back into the earth except for a few non-rottables- foundation stone, corner posts that'd been covered with tar, the odd implement that hadn't been sold for scrap or taken to adorn someone's yard as a quaint novelty. If you thought about it, that was really a mockery of how hard life truly was for the toolmakers and farmers.

Luckily, most people never thought of it, even when painting their new lawn ornaments to match the birdhouses with the doors drawn on- real birds were to be discouraged- they made a terrible mess.

Most folks weren't even aware of the marker, had never seen it much less read it, and came to the park for ball games, festivals, to play on the brand new playground equipment or to splash in the fountains on Wednesdays.

Today, there was a folding table set up next to the marker.

Two young women were glumly packing things up into cloth sacks. Obviously their day had not gone as planned.

She edged closer to the table- not to eavesdrop, that would be rude- but sometimes folding tables in the park meant cookies or something were being given out with whatever pamphlets or beliefs were being peddled.

Woman #1, dressed in blue jeans, sandals, and a tee shirt with
"Urban Gardening- Dig It"
emblazoned on it, was gathering up cheerfully beribboned bundles of packets and gently placing them in the sack.

"Figures. We finally get permission to bring this old garden back into use, and now we can't water it. Why do we even try? No one even came to ASK what we were doing here."

Woman #2, wearing the same uniform, but with cargo pants instead of blue jeans, made a small attempt at humor.

"No- there was that one kid who asked if we had balloons or coupons for Chuck E. Cheese's- remember? He officially proclaimed us 'Lame' before ignoring us."

Chuckling without mirth, the women finished packing up their packets and pamphlets, folded the table and walked off.

Once they had left, she sat on the bench they'd been occupying. She thought it was best that there had been no cookies at this table- from the women's dress and demeanor; they would have been sugarless, chocolateless, tasteless wastes of calories.

And of course, they hadn't seen her.

Sighing, she let her head drop down onto her chest. Her eyes started closing 'just for a rest', but a brightly colored paper caught her attention and she bent over to retrieve the flyer that had been left behind.

City Park Community Garden

**Plots available
Only $50 per year**

**Free Seeds
Free gardening lessons**

Grow your own food

Help Mother Earth

It's Tasty!

She carefully folded the flyer around the bundle of seeds, tied it all together with the colorful ribbon, and slipped it into her pocket.

Pensively, she walked back behind the bench and the metal marker and into the overgrown thicket where the old homestead had been. Closing her eyes, she tried to imagine what it had looked like all those years ago.

In her mind, the house rose again from the foundation stones still in place.

The fence posts ran a helter skelter dot-to-dot around what was left of the barn.

Somewhere in her memory- for her memory was good with things long past- she remembered her grandmother telling her about how farms had been set up 'in the old days'. Something about kitchen gardens…planted between the house and barn.

Something else was niggling at the back of her head. Something about this place. This place. The Place.

She closed her eyes again and breathed deeply. Opened them and looked up, down, into the trees and absorbed their quiet energy.

Quickly now, she paced back and forth, kicking at the weeds as she went. Every so often, her foot would hit something solid- metallic- and she'd uncover it and move it out of the way.

Until she came to a patch of very tall weeds. They were tall because the mowers had gone around them for years. She parted them like window drapery, or the curtain on a stage, and there it was- the water pump.

Rusty, corroded, forgotten, she was surprised that the handle still moved, and she pumped it tentatively.

It screeched. It squawked. Dust and rust rained from the spigot.

Blackish-green musty liquid, oozing age and mildew, glopped out of the spigot.

And then, suddenly and without warning, cascading from the spigot in the ebb and flow of the pump, crystal clear and smelling of life-

Water.

Chapter Two

Food

The menu at the shelter had never been particularly appealing- like most cafeteria-style establishments; the emphasis was more on filling tummies as cheaply as possible and less on things like actual nutrition, and taste.

Now, however, everything had to stretch just that much farther to accommodate the simultaneous influx of new people on a daily basis along with a slow-down in donations both corporate and private- seems everyone was feeling the crunch of the current economy.

In addition to the decline of an already lackluster buffet, mealtimes were made even less satisfying due to the constant running debates as to whether it was worse to have the societal rug pulled out from under you by too much water, or not enough.

Lately there was a whole different brand of newcomers- those who were trying with all their might to wake from this nightmare- they couldn't believe that this venue, this crowd, was their new reality. This type of misfortune only happened to 'other people'. Surely those who were 'one paycheck away from disaster' could never be...them.

And they looked shell-shocked, dazed from pinching themselves, shaking themselves, frantically trying to wake, to turn to their spouse lying in their comfortable bed in their familiar home, to chuckle at the silly dream they'd had. And they became numb with the great weight of the truth that they'd never wake up in that place again. Not physically. Not mentally. Never.

She started to avoid the shelter and spent her time instead over at the old-peoples' dining room.

Three little words gave her this freedom of choice-

"Early Onset Dementia"

was the diagnosis on the medical card she showed to the woman at the door of the senior center- her name had been smudged and couldn't be read, but the photo was unmistakably her, and while it would be overly generous to say she was welcomed with open arms there, at least she was not forbidden admittance- not likely anyway, because of that invisibility thing.

Sitting quietly among other diners, she had nothing to add to the conversation- no family to report on, no complaints (if you can't remember yesterday, there's not much fodder for bemoaning your current troubles).

It really didn't matter- the others were only too willing to give their opinions, their fears, their uneasiness the solidarity of words- nervous moths of thought fluttered between them to be caught, gently examined, and handed back to the owner.

They worried about their families, mostly.

Sons and daughters losing the jobs that defined them as well as supported their lifestyles- homes, cars, country club memberships- the very trappings that they wrapped their lives in were also shed by default, literally.

Grandchildren whose parents could no longer afford to send them off to college competed with their parents for the same service industry jobs just to make ends meet and continue their educations.

Great-grandchildren being born into an uncertain future for the first time in most peoples' memories.

And sitting a little aside from the others, at a table seemingly reserved for those of special distinction, were the grandparents of the young men and women who were serving overseas and facing danger every day.

The occupants of this table were not strangers to war- they'd served in Vietnam, Korea, and Europe back in their day- fighting for freedom, for America, for a concrete cause. But now they were troubled- what exactly were their grandchildren fighting for and against?

No matter what was said, it just didn't ring true this time, and it always came back to one word-
Oil
Oil. In their memories- so not so very long ago- less than 100 years for certain- oil was something you may have burned in your furnace, something you cooked with, something that was nice to have, but not a necessity.

America's love affair with oil had turned a gloriously independent country into a twitching, frantic junkie in less than three generations.

Things hadn't been so bad in a pre-oil world, they thought, remembering lives of comfort and grace.

But they never said it aloud.

It troubled them that their children and grandchildren couldn't even conceive of a life without 'modern conveniences'- would in fact work for years in jobs they hated in order to attain and maintain their image of being civilized.

When had the price of civility surpassed the actual state of being civil- to each other, to their neighbors, to their planet?

On the days when news of a granddaughter or grandson's homecoming was announced, celebration and relieved happiness spread person to person quick and triumphant.

All too often, the news was that another young life had been lost, and mingled with pride in the service and selflessness; there was deep and bottomless mourning at the milestones that would never be seen- marriage, children, happiness, normalcy.

More and more, the happy days became fewer, and the cloud over that table spread across the entire dining room- pressing and heavy.

Finally, she could stand no more.

Although she had no memory of children, or family of any kind, it grieved her to see these grandparents- it wasn't right, wasn't natural- old people die first.

War turned this natural rightness upside down.

To pass the time in her newly-inflicted self-exile, she found herself back at the park, tidying up 'her' place- setting all the metallic things in one pile, fallen branches in another, scraping out a clean patch of dirt a few steps away from the pump with an old hoe that she'd found in the remains of the decrepit barn.

"Well, now what?" she said aloud to herself, surveying the little garden spot she'd made without meaning to.

She'd been working all morning in the sunshine, and her hair was even more disheveled than usual- wisps of silver and copper trailed out from under her ever-present hat.

It was a most excellent hat- large brim to stave off both rain and sun, some sort of canvas material that was light enough to not accumulate heat underneath it, but heavy enough to stand up to daily wear.

It was purple.

And it pleased her to wear it.

The hat was acquired at the same time as the rest of her wardrobe, and from the same place- the county thrift shop. There had been vouchers handed out at the shelter to the permanent residents (the irony of being a permanent resident at a temporary shelter was not lost on her), and a bus had taken them to go 'shopping'.

While the others scanned the racks for name brands or the type of clothing they wore in their former lives, because of her lack of memory of a former life, she was free to choose her clothing in a much more basic way-
-Was the fabric soft and comfortable?
-Did the colors make her happy??
-Were there plenty of pockets???

There must be pockets.

She carried no purse, per se. She had a large duffle type bag that had a very soft padded strap, and in that she carried her two changes of clothing, the few generic toiletries that were handed out free of charge, and several books that she bought with what was left of her voucher money (she was a very thrifty shopper).

One book was a road atlas from several years earlier.

She loved looking at the maps, reading the city names, imagining what the people were like high up in the mountains, or along the beaches. Why were there so many Nashvilles? Who would name a town Neshkoro?

One was a cookbook- one of those fundraiser books with names after each recipe.

She could conjure up what every person looked like from the ingredients they used-how many they cooked for, if they were lean folks or plump from their fondness of sweets.

She wove together the families in her head, and then connected them all under the umbrella of the church the cookbook had been sold by- also seeing with satisfaction the "good works financed by the purchase of this book" being done thousands of miles away in Africa, where the missionaries were.

The most special book was a baby album.

It was filled with photos and notations regarding the first tooth, first day of school, early years of crayoned greeting cards and "I love you Mommy"s, team photos of Little League sports, and one very scary photo from each Halloween.

The pages were blank after age 7.

She was pretty sure that this book came with the others, and it made her sad to think that someone had discarded such a special item.

Pretty sure, but not certain.

Just in case, she liked to think of the child as hers- now all grown up and with a family of his own, and she was very proud of him.

Pockets.

Her clothes all had pockets- the big oversized floweredy shirts, her faded blue jeans, and her sweaters- all had pockets to keep the smaller items safe and secure- a few crumpled dollars from collecting aluminum cans, a tube of chapstick, a comb for her unruly hair, and her medical card that she'd been given when they'd gently but firmly turned her out of the hospital that had been her home since…well, that was the whole trouble, wasn't it?

She couldn't remember.

She pulled the comb through her long hair and tucked it back under her hat, then returned the comb to her pocket. The teeth of the comb caught the side of an envelope- no- several envelopes, and she pulled out the flyer and seed packets still tied in the ribbon.

"Well, how did THAT get there?" she puzzled, having no recollection of picking the items up the previous Sprinkler Day (or was it the Sprinkler Day before that?) She gazed at her newly cleared garden spot, then instinctively turned away from it.

Reading the packets, she carefully cleared areas for each type of seed behind and among the weeds- lettuce here between the foundation stones, beans along what was left of the wooden fence, and so on, until she had planted all but the flower seeds.

These she mixed all together and scattered in her garden plot, smiling at how pretty they would look growing and blooming wild and free- like the old roses and hollyhocks that still came up year after year- outlining in living color where the house had been.

She was hungry.

Washing her hands from the pump, she made her way to the row of stores and restaurants that lined the other side of the street from the park. People were just finishing up their lunches at the café-style tables. As if on cue, men in suits and women in Office Dress gathered up their unfinished meals, tossed them into the trash bins, and headed back to desks, meetings, and an afternoon migraine.

Waiting till most had gone, she sidled up to a bin and carefully plucked out a Styrofoam container that was still almost full of a wonderful chicken salad- meat, greens, veggies, even some fruit and croutons- the abundance was amazing.

That the fork was still inside was a happy bonus.

Behind her a voice shrilled, "MOMMY! That lady is eating from the GARBAGE!" and she startled, almost dropping her meal.

Shushed by her mother, the young child was hurriedly led away- the disapproval at the sight- the sight of HER- palpable.

Not for the first time, she wondered why one of the only times adults acknowledged her existence was to resent that she had the apparent bad taste to exist at all.

Embarrassment washed over her and she had to sit before she fell.

For she was truly embarrassed for that mother- how could you not urge your child to be more considerate of others? And for the child- how sad to grow up thinking that wastefulness of any type was to be not only tolerated, but also encouraged.

She had watched the woman pick at the salad. The woman was young, dressed to the nines, and seemed inordinately but in her circle not unusually concerned with her caloric intake.

When lunch hour was over, the young woman carefully closed up the container and placed it into the bin- none of the food had touched the dirty interior, no one had stubbed out a cigarette in it (she hated when that happened), and it had changed hands just like that, in less time than it had taken to order it, prepare it and deliver it to the original owner. It was good. Clean. Fresh. Food.

Recovered, she took her lunch/dinner back to the park and ate at a private table, alone.

As usual.

Chapter Three

Shelter

During mealtimes at the senior citizens' home, a perky young activities director would announce the many social opportunities for the residents to enjoy.

Mostly her voice was background noise, so much buzzing mulling around and under the real conversation, but one day the buzzing became words and the words piqued her interest.

"The Children's Hospital is looking for volunteers to read stories to the patients- if you're interested, please see me after lunch".

The children loved her.

She had a way of making the fairy tales come to life, the characters all having different voices and expressions- all framed by the purple hat, which became her identity.

"Where's Purple Hat Granny?" the children would wonder to each other if she was even 10 minutes late.

While their parents brought them stuffed animals and the candy stripers brought them treats and the medical staff brought them things that were "good for you- and it'll only hurt for a minute", she brought them treasures from the park- acorns, feathers, pebbles and leaves.

She reported on the magical images in the clouds, the sunshiny warmth of the air, and the call of the common creatures most grownups couldn't hear anymore- squirrels, frogs, cicadas, and sparrows.

All the things they missed by being in the hospital.

She brought the gift of playing outside inside.

And after her reports, she listened to theirs.

Not just the fears and frustrations of being who they were and where they were, but of things remembered- snowflakes turned liquid on a taste bud, baking cookies with their mom, beloved and comical pets at home waiting for them, what they were going to be when they grew up.

Eventually they'd get around to the story.

She picked the stories with care from the library- only those with wild free colors and fabulously delicious words were acceptable. The colors had to leap off the pages and wrap around the children's imaginations while the text burst rolling, roiling, boiling and churning along- carrying them all away triumphantly for just a sliver of time.

Out of the hospital. Away from their hurt, their germs, their helplessness.

While most volunteers came and read their stories, passed around a treat, patted heads and cheeks and were gone in an hour, she spent all afternoon in the company of her children- none of them had anywhere else to be.

She left the hospital each day along with the rush of day staff, relatives and office workers- all with thoughts of the evening ahead of them, while her heart stayed firmly behind.

One evening, returning to the shelter, she noticed not for the first time, the people outside.

Between the floods and the drought, the downturn of the economy and the swelling of unemployment, more and more people were jobless, homeless, hopeless, families stressed and stretched till they broke- and the shards fell sharp and fresh on the doorstep of the shelter.

She had status as 'permanently homeless'- her mental capacity not feeble enough for hospitalization, but not orderly enough for employment, plus she never caused anyone a moment of bother, so her spot in the shelter was secure.

She smiled kindly at the children, who tried valiantly to smile in return. The adults' eyes were fixed inward- unable to look beyond their own troubled thoughts.

Except for one.

She'd smiled at the boy- a young man of about 12- not a little kid anymore yet not quite a teenager, he had his arm around the shoulder of his mother- a gesture both protective and needy.

The corners of the boy's mouth turned up but his eyes were defiant, troubled, ashamed.

Puzzled, she glanced at his mother. The evening shadows were reflected in her tired eyes, her faded hair, and the bruise on her cheek. The shadowed eyes questioned, begged, and pierced straight into her soul with an attack of recognition.

And she knew for sure and for true that this boy, right at the threshold of becoming a man, had had to deny any likeness there was between himself and his father- for one thing the boy would not allow himself to become, was the kind of man who was supposed to be his role model.

And she knew for sure and for true that this woman was herself.

Gently, she touched the boy's arm. "Come with me- it's going to be alright".

Entering the office, she told the secretary, "I won't be needing my place here anymore- my son has come to take me home".

Surprised, but in a hurry to close up the office, the secretary asked, "I thought they said you didn't have a family. Where does your son live?"

"He's from Neshkoro. He's a missionary and has just returned from doing good deeds in Africa. He'll be here in just a little bit to pick me up. I want you to give my spot to these people, please."

And she gathered her few things and left the shelter for the last time.

Although she was tired from her afternoon at the hospital, she appeared fresh and happy when she reported to the evening nurse.

"I'm here to be the overnight volunteer".

The charge nurse looked confused. "I wasn't aware that we were starting an overnight program", she sighed. "They don't tell the night crew ANYTHING, but we surely are glad for your help".

And from that moment on, any child who woke alone and hurting and afraid in the dark had Purple Hat Granny to firmly hold their hand, whisper stories of hope and light, and tuck them in with promises of a better tomorrow.

Chapter Four

Security

Sorting through bags of clothing at the county thrift shop wasn't glamorous work, but someone had to do it- separating the women's from the men's from the children's and then into sizes, making sure the donations were even usable- it was shameful to see bags and bags of clothing torn, stained, even molded. How could civilized people think they were being helpful by 'donating' that mess?

She'd applied for the job the day after she left the shelter. When asked for a form of identification for the application, all she had to offer was her medical card.

The man behind the desk scanned it and said, "Sorry- if you have no permanent address, I can't hire you", and he looked back at his computer screen, dismissively.

"I don't want any money".

He stopped and frowned at her. "What do you mean you don't want money? Everyone wants money".

"Store credit- all I want is store credit. For a few things I need for my home and my children". She stressed the last five words quietly but firmly. Her chin tilted upwards, making her look taller, younger, stronger.

He pondered for a few minutes. Good help was hard to find, most of his crew were young and not very dependable, and the mountains of bags of clothing seemed never to get smaller- they were the one thing that could be counted on- the masses of discarded clothes, black plastic casings stuffed with the innards of closets and drawers- confirming the change of seasons, the growth of children, the call of the mall.

"Fine. Mondays Wednesdays and Fridays- nine till noon. $20 per day store credit. That's all I can offer", he said, and turned back to his work, not wanting to see the relief in her eyes that would reveal the true importance of what he was offering.

She'd moved her duffle bag into the decrepit barn in the park- looking for gardening tools, she'd found a door behind years of cobwebs, dust and the twiney viney thorny plants that grow with abandon where nothing else will. Broken boards and lengths of rusty pipe- discarded remnants of the old homestead were leaning against the door behind the vines, worn, battered yet effective shields.

Luckily, the door opened inwards.

Even more luckily, she was small, slight, and could slip handily behind the vines, which rustled back into place conspiratorially as the door closed again.

The room was small- maybe twelve feet square- and lit by a row of tiny windows high up and facing south. The ceiling was solid thanks to the loft above it. Dust motes swirled and settled on a low wooden workbench, a rolling stool made out of an old tractor seat perched next to it- waiting for the farmer who never came back, and several shelves climbed the wall above it- empty now, except for trails of rodent droppings.

She wet a rag from the pump and set about cleaning off the surfaces. When she was finished, she carefully placed her duffle on the workbench and her books on the shelves.

The sunshine glittered off of the little clouds of dust drifting up and out the open windows- irritated at the intrusion.

Week by week, her life took on a pattern- walking the hospital halls at night, then either sorting clothing or tending her growing plants in the mornings, then napping in the afternoons.

Thanks to her store credit, her room acquired an old futon mattress, a pillow, blankets, a few dishes, more books, even a little area rug, and finally, by a wild stroke of luck, a little one-burner camp stove.

The man who'd 'hired' her saw her delight in the camp stove and after her next shift presented her with a small gift card to a sporting goods store- "Just a little bonus for always being here and being on time," he said matter of factly.

She thanked him and spent the entire card on propane for the stove and a tiny yet bright flashlight and a supply of batteries.

Meanwhile, though no one said anything, it did not escape the notice of the night staff at the hospital that their third shift volunteer worked seven nights a week.

Or that she was apparently the only one in the entire 'program'.

Before long, every night it seemed that one or the other of the medical staff brought "way too much" for their own mid-shift meals, and asked her if she'd help them finish it up.

The parents of the children she comforted began bringing little 'thank you' packages for her- fancy little baskets wrapped in lacy cellophane containing teas, cocoa, nuts, cookies and soup mixes.

She was grateful for it all, but cherished most the cards from the children- and she carefully placed them between the empty pages of the baby album.

She was busier now than she could ever remember being, and she drifted off to her afternoon naps tired, sleeping on used bedding in an abandoned barn, everything she owned within reach.

And she marveled at how very rich she was.

Chapter Five

Health

She felt good.

True, she spent every night in the oddly antiseptic yet unhealthy air of the hospital, but the rest of the time she was outside- either in the large three sided warehouse sorting clothing or at home- inside and out filled with the same freshness.

She didn't miss the close, pre-breathed atmosphere in the shelter or the senior citizen's dining room that smelt faintly but certainly of urine and whatever had been the last meal served.

In her garden she could take deep breaths and feel the oxygen entering her lungs, and then breathe out- returning the carbon dioxide to the trees and plants surrounding her, in a never-ending exchange of life.

Her diet was far better than it had been at the troughs of humanity- even the days she ate nothing but leftovers from in front of the restaurants. Augmenting the leftovers taken and those given at the hospital, plus the small gifts from the patients' families, her hidden vegetables were producing for her- not bumper crops to be sure, but enough to add a small salad, a few beans, fresh herbs.

Drinking water came from the pump- ice cold and slightly metallic tasting- of iron, of the earth, of minerals. After a very short time she found she almost gagged at the water from a drinking fountain, city water laced with fluoride and chlorine.

Her daily washing was done from the pump as well, a cup of boiling water heated on her little stove added to a pot of cold water made for comfortable bathing, luxurious with soaps and shampoos from the little gift baskets.

She walked or rode the city bus wherever she went, and only felt uneasy in the late evenings, because the sun went down long before her time to officially be at the hospital.

She started going right before dark and sitting in the surgical waiting room- fetching coffee, sharing a newspaper or just quietly reading in the corner.

Worry about a child in surgery either made her more invisible to folks, or they were attracted to her- she was someone they could talk to- stories about their temporarily unconscious loved ones flowed strong and true from their hearts.

Spoken aloud, these stories were ropes that bound them to the patient- and they clung to them lest the patient drift away and not come back.

The stories were woven through with homes, vacations, children and grandchildren- the very fibers holding these families together and she couldn't help but wonder if somewhere she'd had all these, any of these, ever.

So she was a good listener, and she prayed with them, and her heart lifted sincerely every time the nurse came out to say, "You can see him now- he did just fine".

No matter how long the surgery had been, they were revived, refreshed by those words, and their elation pulled them out of the waiting room, away from her and back into their lives.

She looked after them and tried to imagine what it would be like to have a life like that- to have such a rope to cling to, and to know that there was someone at the other end of it.

Chapter Six

Community

It didn't take very long before her little home had enough amenities to be comfortable, but she had grown accustomed to working at the thrift store, so she continued to show up.

Her store credits accumulated and she kept her ears open.

There was an article in the newspaper- the stressful times springing from the bad economy meant that the battered women's shelter was filled to overflowing, and it desperately needed dishes and bedding- things for broken families to start new lives…

…And a large box of dishes and bedding was left on the doorstep the next week.

On the news, the reporter said that in these sad times brought on by so many people being unemployed, more and more children needed clothing for school…

…And a large box of sturdy and serviceable clothing was left on the doorstep of one of the elementary schools.

The fire department advertised an extra special plea for their Toys For Tots campaign- corporate donations were way down because of the low profits this last year had brought…

…And a large box of unbroken and clean toys was left in front of the fire station.

This scenario played over and over again- every week or so, somewhere in town, there would be a 'special delivery' by an anonymous donor, who made no bold orchestrated blasts of a charitable nature- no announcements of giving, no interviews, nothing to publicly display the filling of private need.

The gifts were small, but timely, and thoughtful, and perfect.

Society in general still seemed oblivious to the very real needs of a lot of its members- part of being able to maintain a semblance of sanity is the ability to be just enough of an empath to be genuinely concerned about others, but have a large enough measure of distraction to keep from getting too close, too involved, to not get burned by the same flame.

Because
Bad Thing + (someone very different from me) = Sad, but oh well
But
Bad Thing + (random person who could even be ME) = Terror

So, a goodly amount of Community Service was committed at arms' length- as if Bad Thing Germs can be caught by association.

Large measures of distraction were very easy to come by- everyone knew of someone who was laid off, facing or in foreclosure, in the midst of a break-up or breakdown, and the fingers of blame pointed fast and furious-

The politicians, the conservatives, the liberals, the (fill in the blank with the name of any population that isn't…yours), the younger generation, the older generation, God, Satan, Mother Nature, Father Time, all were hauled out, trussed up, interrogated, embraced and then discarded.

And the Bad Things kept on coming on and ever closer to Home.

For a long time, for most people, this remained an abstract distraction.

Most people got up every morning, fed their families, took a shower, got in their cars and went to work. After work there was money for groceries, gas, utilities, and some extracurricular activities for the children, or for themselves if they didn't have offspring. Offspring are expensive.

Looking back on their own childhoods, it did seem that it was simpler when they were young- in those times moms generally didn't go to work, and people were comfortable in their little houses where the children played ball in the streets and built clubhouses in empty lots. It was a world where Men were not from Mars and Women were not from Venus. Boys WERE from Jupiter, but only because they were stupit-er.

Somehow, things had sped up, gotten more complex as their tasks were made easier via technological wonders. Things they used to have to do themselves- usually in cooperation or at least the company of other humans, were accomplished by a machine, and they were free to do…what?

In an amazing leap backwards, instead of taking their newly freed time and spending it with other humans in humanlike pursuits- organic things like touching, thinking, talking, cooking, eating, playing, loving

They took that free time having machines afforded them and

Spent it with other machines.

Televisions, computers, things with wheels, things that plugged into the wall, the car, their ears.

It was wondrous- the Internet especially brought them in contact with millions of people and ideas that they'd never have met in real life. Email, Gmail, Facebook and forums for everything from kittens to automatic weapons brought them together- united in common interests and beliefs, without ever having to meet in person.

The family dinner table was replaced by everyone eating in their respective rooms in front of their respective screens- TV, computer, video game…

News and news-like headlines from around the planet replaced the local newspaper and coffee shop talk, and many times they knew things that were going on thousands of miles away while their neighbors were in trouble- quietly out of sight.

They weren't bad people. They were good people who were busy working, busy raising their families the way they thought they were supposed to.

That had gotten harder to do lately- prices rose while wages stagnated, so they started working harder, longer, sometimes 6 or 7 days a week at two or three different jobs and that left them exhausted.

At the end of the day they were exhausted and they fell into their chairs in front of the TV, in front of the computer, to feel like they were informed, connected, up to date.

And they gave as they could to Save the Whales and to their church missionaries for children in Africa and they bought endless streams of popcorn and wrapping paper and frozen cookie dough to support their children's school teams and clubs.

They were trying to do right.

They did care about their communities.

But they had painted themselves into a technological corner and clung to the carefully manicured illusion that their world was safe, and clean, and secure,

That if they could only hold the right jobs, believe the right things, keep on the proper paths and not color outside of the lines

They wouldn't end up homeless

Living in a park

And eating from the trash.

Chapter Seven

Faith

The times she spent praying with families in the surgical waiting room seemed awkward at first.

She didn't attend church- with no memory of her past, she really didn't know what she was supposed to believe, how she had been raised, which god to follow.

The prayers of the families who had little ones ling still under bright lights consisted of many words, but one message
"Please"
No matter the name on the door of their place of worship, the sequence of the services or the attire of the men and women directing the churches and guiding the parishioners, what holidays were celebrated or historical events commemorated, each and every person in that waiting room sent one word forth into the cosmos, up to heaven, appealing to an entity that could make things right again
"Please"

So even though she had no official religious affiliation, that one word held meaning for her, and she was only too happy to add her energy to it- one more earnest current wafting one tiny feather of a word upwards, out of their hands and the hands of the doctors and into the care of Someone who could make it all better.

Things happened.

Unfair things happened all the time, and she knew it from her own circumstances and those of all the people at the shelter and all the people in the old folks' home and without question for all the children in the hospital.

Now that she had bookshelves, her personal library was growing, and one of the books she'd added was a dog-eared and worn Bible.

Sometimes, not often, but sometimes, Someone didn't hear the prayers, somehow they prayer got lost, misdirected, delayed or otherwise detained, and the nurse was not smiling when she came into the waiting room.

Those families visibly shrank in front of her eyes- the actual mass of each individual sucking inwards and becoming smaller at the loss of another's soul from their midst.

And they allowed the nurse to lead them out of the waiting room- holding onto each other while the rope of stories connecting them to their lost one trailed behind them, frayed and broken.

The first few nights this happened, she did not tend to "her" children, but instead returned to her little room, empty and full of questions.

She opened the bible and turned on her little flashlight- a tiny beacon in the darkness.

From listening to various preachers in the shelter and at the park, she knew somewhere in that book comfort was found, and answers- if read correctly and with enough faith, all would be revealed and peace could be had. You could find God.

But although she read it cover to cover, and although his name was on every page, she never could find God in the book.

It was a nice enough book. It had history and adventure, poetry, and laws, happy endings and righteous punishments.

Very definitely a book ABOUT God, but she clearly felt that

God did not live there.

She went to church.

There were any number of churches within sight of the park- lining the streets with steeples and stained glass and promises of salvation.

She'd sit in a back pew, and peace permeated the congregation. The music was uplifting, joyous, somber or reverent depending on the hymns and the instruments engaged.

The sermons were comforting, humorous, stern or informative depending on the scripture it was based on and the mood and demeanor of the preacher. And the underlying current of all the sermons was how important it was- your very life and all that came afterwards, depended on whether or not you could find God.

People surrounded her- good people who cared for the poor in the community and gave canned food for holiday baskets and maybe even served up turkey dinners at the shelters.

Much time was spent in the planning of doing good deeds and the reports of good deeds accomplished,

And even though no one looked at her with disapproval or dislike, neither did they look at her with warmth and concern.

Because she continued to be invisible.

So she wandered in and out of the churches, never feeling reviled, but never feeling welcomed, and she couldn't help but feel that even thought the church buildings offered comfort to the believers and gave solid walls to their Faith

God didn't live there either.

She stopped looking for God, and concentrated instead on her life and the things she tended to and cared about.

Her little patch of flower seeds had grown up and was blooming.

The disturbed soil turned over by the rusted hoe had welcomed not only the respectable tame seeds in their labeled and ribbon-wrapped packets, but also those that were planted by the wind, that gathered and stowed away on the hem of her frayed blue jeans, that ingloriously plummeted from the sky encased in bird droppings.

Despite the diversity of their beginnings, every seed became a plant, every plant became a flower, and every flower was beautiful.

Clovers and marigolds, daisies and dandelions, framed and supported by foliage leafy or fernlike, spiky or furry, and right in the center, if she looked with her soul instead of her eyes, there he was-

God.

So she carefully pressed flowers in between the pages of the bible and she returned to walk the halls of the hospital at night- feeling better now that God wasn't lost anymore.

Part Two

2010

"Extremely Perishable"

<u>Chapter Eight</u>

<u>Water</u>

The sprinklers never did turn back on in the park on Wednesdays.

The official note announcing the temporary discontinuation of sprinkler fun turned yellow, wrinkled up at the edges and one day blew away, torn loose from its tape by apathy.

But only she seemed to notice.

Not many people came to the park anymore- at least not anyone who drove there.

Gasoline was expensive, groceries became expensive- commercial trailers didn't go anywhere anymore unless they had a return load, and even then the expenses of running a big rig put a lot of independent drivers out of business.

Because gas was expensive, school supplies and clothing became expensive- anything, actually, that had to travel from Point A to Point B absorbed and then redistributed the extra expense in getting it to its point of usage.

That gasoline was important to maintaining a civil society was a given- more money was printed, earmarked and allotted to finding sources for oil or any type of energy making substance- the country was gasping, greedy, needy for it.

So even when the children asked, "Mommy- why can't we go to sprinkler day anymore?" the issue was not about water and why it wasn't spurting in a crystal geyser at the park, the issue was, "Honey- we can't waste gas on that sort of thing- here- play in the hose for a while".

And when the newspapers and television stations proclaimed that all watering of any type was banned because of the need for water conservation, the children wondered why they weren't playing in the hose anymore.

And their parents became irritable when asked about it.

So they stopped asking.

Far under the surface of the earth, below the park, below her garden, below the little underground stream her pump tapped into that still flowed happily- so small no one else had bothered with it- below even the layer below that one, the enormous aquifer was quietly dying.

On the surface of the planet, the citizens ran to and fro, back and forth to work, to school, to church, to meetings regarding the shortage of gasoline and how to maintain a modern life in the face of the current unemployment and uncertainty.

There was sounding and drilling, and the earth shook, shuddered in the throes of progression, or what passed for progression.
>   Humans believe activity = progress
If they can just keep moving, keep busy enough, keep up, keep one step ahead, they can keep doing what they've been doing all along even if it's clearly the wrong thing.

There was talk and much posturing about alternatives to gasoline and oil. And they all sounded terrific except that just like it takes money to make money, it takes energy to produce energy, and the energy available to produce this alternative energy came from oil.

Parts, pieces components and even the manuals on how to install them, all cast from the same oil-soaked molds that were being reviled, defiled and exiled in the minds of the citizenry.

Even those who recognized that what they were doing 'now' was unsustainable insisted on asking, "What do we do NEXT?"

And the scientists and the manufacturers and the marketers were only too willing to answer the question with new toys, new answers, new gadgets for doing things just different enough to appear clearly innovative, but that acted in essentially the same old familiar comfortable wasteful ways.

When mommy held up the new light bulb that was curlicue and cost $5 instead of the old fashioned round globe that cost $1,

The child asked, "Why don't we just turn off the lights?"

When daddy pulled into the driveway with the brand new electric car that cost $30,000 instead of the exact same car that drank gasoline and cost $15,000

The child asked, "Why don't we just drive less?"

The children knew instinctively and the old people knew anecdotally, the question should not have been

"What do we do NEXT?"

It should have been

"How far back do we need to go to find sanity?"

And the rain stayed away from the parched areas, and the hurricanes whipped the soggy areas into swirling gurgling mires, and everyone wondered why the winds were changing and Tornado Alley was shifting and there were earthquakes where there had never been earthquakes before.

Sinkholes opened up and swallowed whole cars- but usually not expensive electric ones.

The frenzied quest for oil continued unabated and each isolated pocket that was sounded from between the folds of the planet was sucked dry, stripped dry, the sides scraped with a mining spatula before the equipment moved on- tools of the parasites.

Rivers and springs, lakes and streams, sank lower and lower and finally disappeared, but only the fish and the lily pads noticed- the people were all too busy worrying about oil.

As long as the water turned on when a faucet was twisted, everything was fine.

The underground aquifers had seemed so immense- ocean sized pools of water literally chillin' underground till they needed them, had been tapped for drinking, bathing, industry, agriculture, anything that required or desired water was obliged by the aquifers.

For years and decades and generations, the aquifers supplied, and were recharged by falling rains, by melting snow, just as had been done for many more centuries than the humans had been there.

That something as small and insignificant as one species could tip the balance was unthinkable, unimaginable and impossible.

So impossible that most grownups never even gave it a first thought, much less a second.

"Mommy- where did the frogs go? The pond is all dry and the frogs are gone- where did they go?"

Distracted by her cell phone and her People magazine, the child's mother said "That's nice, honey".

The child turned to the invisible woman who sat next to them on the park bench.

"Where did they go? Their legs are so short and they need water".

She looked at the child.

"I don't know, dear. I worry about them, too".

Chapter Nine

Food

Food was expensive, and everyone blamed the price of gasoline for the rising cost of feeding their families, but even though they were mostly correct, their assumptions stopped short of all the actual reasons.

That it took more money to get food from where it was grown to the dinner table was indisputable.

But down on the farm, it went much deeper than that.

Not only did tractors run on gasoline, but the fertilizer and weed killers and bug poisons that were needed to grow the massive specialty crops America literally ran on were petroleum-based as well. The very food put into their mouths was grown in, soaked with, harvested by and transported via oil.

Just a few generations ago, people knew where their food came from because most of their meals were locally grown, and exotic things like bananas and chocolate were rare treats not included in the daily diets of people living far from the equator.

Every location has different soil, different rainfall, different seasonal variations and each regional neighborhood sprouted and nourished edibles whose names were as delicious as themselves.

Boon County White corn, Eden Gem muskmelon, Kentucky Wonder string beans, Crimson Cushion tomatoes- food had a history richer than a brand name, and traveling from place to place brought surprise and wonder with a trip to the market of new shapes, colors and flavors for common veggies and fruits.

As the food chain became mechanized, food had to become less about being edible and more about being uniform parts that fit into the harvesting equipment and packages and less about being flavorful and more about surviving shipping and cold storage.

A whole new science evolved devoted to re-inventing something as basic as a seed, and this Brave New Agriculture swallowed farms whole, devoured soil nutrients voraciously and inhaled water by the lakeful.

Far beyond anything science fiction writers had ever dreamt of, plants became engineered, enhanced, able to withstand the poisons that killed the 'weeds', launched past the messy casualness of cross-pollination to produce living things that were so specialized they were trademarked and protected by 'terminator' genes- every generation was the only one and plants literally committed suicide after producing their one crop of food- the very fruits of their labor sterile.

Animals, too- livestock, were managed and mutated in much the same way.

Creatures who had evolved to fit seamlessly into their environments were tweaked here, trimmed there, meat production and ability to stand confinement bred in while instinct and brains were bred out, leaving only faded caricatures crowded and cramped into feedlots and pens- erasing all genetic memory of being herds and flocks.

Conditions were depressing to deadly. The livestock were fed steroids to make them grow quickly and antibiotics to keep them alive in their unsanitary surroundings until they were killed and sent to be processed.

The meat was soaked in anti-bacterial solution, which was then (mostly) washed off before packaging.

Dairy products weren't much better. Growth hormones were given to the cows to increase their production, and the milk was pasteurized to the point of needing to have nutrients added back into it. Artificially manufactured nutrients.

Only years afterwards were things noticed like the erratic growth (or not) of children, higher instances of sterility in men, increased 'female problems' in women, and cancer running rampant throughout the population.

The industry made attempts to clean up their acts- not so much out of concern for public safety as fear over being sued, but the end sometimes justifies the means.

The average shopper at the average grocery store didn't think much about any of this- they gathered up familiar food items in their carts- shrink wrapped dyed meats, ultra-pasteurized vitamin-added dairy, fruits and veggies that were more wax than food substance and tasted it, cereals in festive but unnatural blues and reds, and bread with the consistency of puffed pre-masticated sawdust- only not as appetizing.

Standing in line in the checkout never once did it occur to any of them that this abundance, this entire building full of foodstuffs, was more precarious than a snowball in Hades.

One bad gasoline strike and their stores would be empty.

One bad crop and the entire country's corn or potato or soybean supply would be gone- where once because of the regional differences there were hundreds of varieties of each as a safety net, there were now three, yes three varieties of each.

In spite of the massive doses of antibiotics given, disease sprang up in the feedlots and pens, and though they were managing to keep ahead of it, barely, they were one big outbreak away from having no meat- just like the food plants, the food animals were in a quandary- the gene pool ridiculously tiny considering the millions of swimmers.

Lately, there had also been a disturbing occurrence of germs that were not species specific- where in the past, with very few exceptions (like Rabies), cows got cow diseases, birds got bird diseases and so on.

Viruses jumped from livestock species to humans where they were in close constant contact, and then, rarely but annoyingly, from human to human.

Sensing the need to be more aware of their food, some folks took up gardening, with varying degrees of satisfaction and success.

Pockets of heritage seeds were discovered, saved and shared. These too, had various ratios of work expended to food content harvested depending on how much homework the gardener had done- being careful to only use varieties that had originally been in their region. Because of their localized beginnings, the heritage varieties were both more hardy and more particular.

Farmers Markets sprang up and offered tasty nutritious alternatives peddled in the sunshine and it was a stark contrast to the row upon row of identical vegetative matter stocked in the conditioned air of the supercenters.

People began tasting, enjoying, preferring.

This alarmed the big Name Brand companies and they fought back.

Reports of dirt, can you imagine? DIRT on the farmers market foods were published and advertised, And in the dirt lurked germs both disgusting and lethal- e-coli, salmonella, botulism- sure the food at the farmers market was appealing in a risky edgy sort of way, but if you wanted your families to be SAFE, you shopped at the supercenter.

People hesitated, sighed deeply, and turned away from the farmers market.

Some families with large yards decided to have a more hands-on affair with their eggs and dairy products and got small flocks of hens and a dairy goat or two.

There's something very fulfilling and rewarding about animal husbandry, especially when the end result is good healthy food on your family's table, and "The Urban Farm" was catching on.

This alarmed the big Name Brand companies and they fought back.

Bird Flu! Bird Flu coming from nasty infected wild birds flying over hen houses and yards and dropping lethal bombs of virus-laden poo was threatening the health of the entire human population with the ability to wipe out life as they knew it.

The only safe way to raise poultry is inside fully enclosed barns- something best left to the professional poultry farmers.

People hesitated, sighed deeply, and turned away from their chickens.

Then Mad Cow Disease and Swine Flu reared their ugly infectious heads and the people were told, "In order for your food supply to be safe, we need to institute a program limiting all food animals to be raised on registered properties and tag each and every creature bound for your family's table so we can track food from farm to plate. Because we want you to be safe. Of course you may keep your dairy goats as long as you pay to be registered, pay to have your animal(s) tagged, and tell us each and every time your animal leaves your property. And by the way- do you have a mechanical pasteurizer for that raw milk?"

The people hesitated, sighed deeply, and turned away from their dairy goats.

And even though it meant that the people were still locked into a very limited and dangerously tenuous food supply
    There was much joy in big Name brand land.

Meanwhile, things had begun to go awry in the endless fields of trouble-free hybrid herbicide-resistant crops.

Plants that had been genetically engineered to be resistant to specific poisons that would kill weeds were having the extreme social bad taste to actually cross-pollinate with those same weeds.

In Nature, this is called evolution.

In Agriculture, this is called problematic.

Pesticides had been sprayed on, poured on, doused on food- although 'poisoning the vegetables' sounded faintly alarming, so it was referred to as 'crop dusting'- "Oh, nothing. We're just dusting the crops- to keep them clean for the children you know…"

Years of this practice had accomplished four things-

They were able to keep the bugs out of the food, mostly.

They were able to keep from poisoning the children, mostly.

The offending bugs evolved to become resistant to the poisons.

The beneficial bugs weren't so lucky.

Crop production dropped. The farmers looked to the agricultural extension agents who looked to the seed companies who looked to the scientists who got out their recipes for fertilizers, poisons and seed mutations.

But it didn't help.

Honey producers were concerned. Their production was down- the bees were not going out to gather pollen and coming back to the hive. They were going out to gather pollen and not coming back.

The bee farmers thought it might be a fungus and medicated all the bees.

The bee farmers thought it might be their stock and re-queened all the hives.

The bee farmers looked to the agricultural extension agents who said, "The scientists are working on it".

The scientists worked tirelessly and around the clock to conjure up a better fertilizer, a stronger poison, new super-plants and a tonic that would cure what was ailing the little honey-machines.

And the children in their classrooms learned important lessons about the dark days of DDT- shielded their eyes from the photos of dead and deformed hatchling condors and eagles who'd been driven to the brink of extinction by the inadvertent actions of humans.

Teachers finished the lesson with encouraging and comforting words- things were different now, scientists were more careful now, things like that would never happen again.

Reassured, the children were served their lunches that each day were just different ways of cooking the same 3 varieties of corn, the same 3 varieties of potatoes, and the same 3 varieties of tomatoes, with a side of some sort of livestock that was raised up by the millions all over the country- one or two bloodlines of each.

The food was harvested, stored and moved thousands of miles before reaching point of use, then stored again till eaten- all by oil.

Their food chain had once been thousands of links all working together, strengthened by variety.

In an effort to feed the most people in the most efficient manner, all those links had been welded together to form one solid bar.

And where a chain flexes and moves under pressure, a solid bar breaks.

She was reading a little book she'd bought when the library had its $1 sale of books that weren't very popular. It was called "Edible Weeds" and she was finding it interesting that a lot of the plants she'd been pulling out of her garden were actually healthy for you and good to eat.

She glanced up as she heard running footsteps.

The little boy tugged at his father's sleeve.

"Daddy- look- it's a bee. He was just lying on the ground. He's not dead, but he looks sick. What can we do to help him?"

"Put it down, son. Before it stings you. It's just a bug."
                "It's not important."

Chapter Ten

Shelter

The cost of heating and cooling homes was rising at the same alarming speed of everything else that slid along the fossil fuel lifeline.

Architects and builders answered the call for more efficient housing in the usual manner- by introducing new materials, new innovations, new building designs that relied on new technology all run on and supplied by their old friend Oil.

Larger, tighter, more airtight than ever before, the New and Improved houses soon covered the landscape like a rash.

From the tip of their asphalt shingles through the rolls of pink insulation in the attic, running along their drywalled, housewrapped, vinyl sided sides and super-sealed windows with the insulated plastic blinds, to the stain resistant flame resistant carpeting running from wall to painted wall, these houses were enormous Tupperware habitations- up to and including the gentle reassuring 'burp' of a seal when the doors closed behind the occupants- protecting them from the dangers outside.

Energy efficient homes filled with Energy Star rated appliances saved money on heating and cooling bills, saved water in washing machines and dishwashers, and the homeowners felt proud that they were contributing to the solution, and not the problem.

Oddly enough, they were also feeling a little woozy. The incidence of headaches, asthma, allergies, all rose and kept rising, and people assumed the culprit was from outside- pollution either natural or man-made.

They snugged up even tighter into their climate controlled cocoons.

The super-efficient super-powerful material used inside the new homes gave them that 'new car smell', which is, unfortunately, the odor of all the preservative toxins used in the manufacturing process.

Proud new owners of these homes were told, "Congratulations! Enjoy your new home- here's a nice potted plant to start decorating. Oh. And by the way, you may want to add at least one large live plant to every room and leave the doors open as much as possible for the first 6 months or so- to keep you and your children from dying due to the poisons that everything in your home is steeped in. Thanks again- and have a great life!"

"Sick Home Syndrome" is what it was called, and it was a malady directly caused by the sealing off of the insides of their homes from the outsides.

Where previous generations had screened windows and doors, took their rugs outside to beat with brooms and no matter the weather, 'aired out' the house once a week when they did their scrubbing and cleaning, these new houses were built to be shut up and remain shut up.

Being tightly sealed and smothered in insulation made for very efficient heating and cooling because the air inside stayed inside, with no annoying infiltration from the outside temperatures.

The air inside became stale, stagnant, breathed, re-breathed and grew mildews and molds with alarming efficiency- the vents and filters of the heating and air conditioning units acted as incubators.

Beneath the houses, inside the air-tight basements, radon built up, and people installed radon alarms along with the smoke alarms their insurance companies still required even though there was very little lumber in the houses and all the soft materials were impregnated with flame retardant.

Every once in a while, one of these super-sealed house balloons filled with natural gas…and exploded.

Not wanting to live in explosive giant Tupperware that made them sick, the people demanded answers.

And once again, the scientists and businessmen rallied round with answers aplenty- new fixes to new problems instead of stepping back a bit, opening the places back up again and literally letting a breath of fresh air in.

"Fresh Air Exchange Systems" mechanically sucked in and filtered air from outside, pushed it through the houses, and exhaled out the old air- giant iron lungs.

Of course, this negated some of the savings from sealing the houses so tightly, but the people weren't sick anymore, so it was well worth it.

In the summertime, if there was a power outage due to a thunderstorm or other act of Nature, the people languished- there was no way to escape the heat naturally- the builders had shunned age old rules of cross-ventilation and positioning- they'd become smug in the assumption of conditioned air.

Every summer a number of weak or elderly people quietly, silently slipped away in the heat- too frail to leave their houses, or too afraid of a high electric bill to turn on the air conditioning unit.

Sometimes the windows were never meant to be opened, but even those that opened more likely than not were 'dead end' openings- the wall opposite had no door or other window to facilitate a breeze.

And every winter the power would flicker and go out due to some weather event- ice or snow- and people couldn't cook, or wash, or see in the dark, or keep warm.

To "shelter" is to keep safe, and comfortable, and secure. Shelter by definition should be not only supportive but also self-supporting.

Old houses, old shelters, did this- they lit with the sun using well-placed windows; they had fireplaces to gather around for warmth, and basements to retreat to from the summer heat. Every room had proper cross-ventilation, and porches embraced them- an invitation to the inhabitants to go outside, and neighbors to come in.

The new structures lined subdivision streets- each hermetically sealed carton containing a single family- keeping them segregated and guarding them from the riotous mess of the natural world.

The little boy ran his toy trucks up and down the planks of the park bench, giving each one a rumbling engine voice as only little boys can do. When he got to the end of the bench, he sighed, and turned the trucks around again.

Every few minutes he turned his attention to his open can of pop and snack sized bag of chips- it was 10am.

He was very clean. More clean than was good for a little boy.

He smelled of bug repellant and sunscreen.

She waited for a pause in the snacking and playing, then said quietly, "You know- there's a sand box right next to us- wouldn't your trucks like driving in the sand box better than on the bench?"

Longingly gazing at the undisturbed dunes clearly in need of tiny truck tracks, he sighed again and replied, "I can't. My mom won't let me get dirty."

Chapter Eleven

Security

The history books would read that one day they woke up and the world was no longer safe.

And everyone could remember that day and the days that followed- on the TV screen, every channel and every minute of every day for an eternity- and much longer than that for those who lost loved ones, the towers exploded, burst into flames and crumbled, burying an entire society's sense of safety under tons of smoldering horrifying rubble.

That was the Big Answer to the question "When did you stop feeling safe?"

Nine Eleven

And in a Big Way, that was correct. Nine Eleven showed them that their country was not impervious, not the Golden Child of the Universe that they'd been taught. All those images from far away across oceans- of wars and devastation and fear could very easily be…here. Were here. Present tense.

But somehow, somewhere now impossible to pinpoint, the feeling of safety had been eroding long before Nine Eleven.

When did they stop leaving houses and cars unlocked?

When did they start thinking a home security system was more than a big yellow Labrador sleeping on the sofa while they were at work?

When did schools stop letting students go to the restroom unattended, or enter the premises without first ducking through a metal detector?

When did the phrase "A stranger is just a friend un-met" become replaced with admonitions to avoid, nay, RUN from "The Friendly Stranger"?

There was a time not so long ago- just a mere generation back- where the world was there for children to run wild in- to explore, unsupervised, from dawn till well after dark on all but a school night. Alone or in groups, children got dirty, made up rules and games and elaborate dramas and it was considered very odd (and not in a good way) if a child remained within sight of his or her yard at any time unless they were being punished- literally grounded.

When did it begin? This push to make the world around us less casual, less free, less dirty, less…human?

Everywhere, everyplace they went and everything they did, even the food on their plates and the clothes on their backs was evaluated for how safe it was- dangers real and imagined, common or fluke of nature were addressed and adjustments made to all aspects of their lives.
                    Just to be safe.
So they ate sterile foods soaked in preservatives and sealed in layer after layer of plastic and cardboard.

Their children were doused with sunscreen and bug repellent to leave the house and at the end of the day they were scrubbed with anti-bacterial soap.

Everything from baseballs to Barbie to Styrofoam cups of coffee warned to be careful- given the right circumstance, those items (actually pretty much ANY items) could maim or kill them.

Their cars had alarms for theft and calming motherly voices that would talk to them- give them directions if they got lost or soothe them till an ambulance arrived if they had a wreck.

Schools looked less like libraries and more like prisons.

And yet, instead of becoming safer, their world became more dangerous.

Possessions were not respected, but stolen or ruined.

Children were harmed by not only Friendly Strangers, but more likely people they knew and trusted.

Adults hurt each other.

Children hurt each other.

No one trusted anyone. Or anything.

Oh, people had family, and people had friends, but even this closeness was reserved and guarded.

The idea of just walking into someone's home because you were friend or family was unthinkable anymore.

There were boundaries to respect and privacies to maintain.

Just to be safe.

People were afraid. Afraid of dangers seen and unseen and every time they turned around they were reminded just how unsafe they were.

Right alongside the weather forecast and the traffic alerts on the news were colors- white, yellow, orange or red- different levels of perceived danger from terrorists.

Being cautious was no longer enough and they looked for dangers and threats in everything and everyone.

The measures of safety became shackles of isolation.

Returning home one morning, she noticed the door to her room was just a little ajar, and she hesitated for a moment before entering carefully. She was reasonably certain that no one knew where she lived, and reasonably certain that no one ever followed her or paid any attention to her at all.

By current standards of caution, she should've not entered. She should've alerted the authorities who would've locked her up for trespassing and called the park crew to nail the door shut to avoid further 'problems'.

So instead, she opted for reasonable certainty and slipped into her room.

Lying on her bed, long body curled with a whiskered nose forming the bottom of a question mark, was a little dog.

The dog was black and white spotted, bewhiskered and eyebrowed, very old, and very comfortable.

It peered at her through cataracts, and its tail swish swish swished on the bed. It didn't seem lost, didn't seem frightened, didn't seem uncared for.

It looked for all the world like it was simply waiting patiently, and it was old enough to know that waiting on a comfortable bed beat the stuffing out of waiting out in the big world, alone.

"Well, I certainly know that feeling", she whispered to the dog and patted it on the head.

Even though she couldn't remember her own name, she named the dog. In one of her books about plants, she found a wildflower indigenous to that area of the country. Small, unspectacular, yet beautiful just because of its specialness, she decided to call the dog by the same name- Tahoka Daisy.

Daisy accompanied her during the day, and slept in their room while she was gone at night- being deaf, there was little chance of her barking, and being old, she had the wisdom to know that most things aren't worth getting all worked up about.

They were two old gals of unknown origin keeping each other company, and that was enough for both of them. Just to have companionship, just to be warm and dry and fed- the type of security that can't be attained through fear.

>Just to be safe.

She was a little curious though, because watching the dog twitch in her sleep she could see Daisy reliving a past life remembered- every squirrel chased, every seagull that got away, every moment of every day being loved.

So just as she thought of the boy in the baby book as her own, she took Daisy's past life filled with happiness and love as her own- and Daisy didn't mind at all.

Walking through the park on a sunny afternoon, she and Daisy stopped to watch a young child picking dandelions.

Chubby fingers clutched a quickly wilting bouquet of earthbound sunshine and the little girl ran to her mother and offered up her gift. She paused to catch her breath and her mother interjected reproachfully.

"Honey- those are just weeds. By the time we get them home they'll be dead and ugly. Put them down and lets go wash your hands- no telling what's all over them".

The child trailed after her mother by just a few steps, and paused long enough to pet the old dog and share what she had wanted to say with someone who smiled at her and would listen.

"We learned how to spell colors today in pre-school. This is y-e-l-l-o-w. You can keep it if you want", and she proudly presented the crumpled blossom.

Her mother whirled around and snatched the girl by the hand, the rest of the dandelions scattering broken to the ground. She was alarmed and on guard, for of course, she hadn't even seen anyone else there.

"What have I told you about talking to strangers?" the fear in her mother's voice brought tears peeking to the corners of the child's eyes.

They disappeared into the restroom briskly, and although she wanted to look back, to wave or smile, the little girl didn't dare.

The worn bible was filled now with flowers both wild and domestic in various stages of preservation, but she carefully wrapped the little y-e-l-l-o-w dandelion in cellophane before closing the book on it.

Just to be safe.

Chapter Twelve

Health

They were the most affluent society the earth had ever seen, which was surprising since their health was so poor.

No one was more surprised than they themselves, and they worried and grumbled and wondered aloud at how many doctors there were, how much magic science was capable of, how many dollars they spent paying premiums to the Health Care Industry and yet people got sick of things they never used to, and died in spite of medical and mechanical intervention.

That a lot of the problems were directly traceable to their society's attempts at cleanliness and safety was a troubling thought that niggled at the backs of their minds.

That's mostly as far as it went though, and they accepted with gratitude and a smile the status quo for health care as they would accept a god-awful fruitcake from a beloved aunt- as something offered up with thought and care and their very best interests in mind.

And it never occurred to them that the farther they moved from a messy, chaotic way of living that exposed them to quiet and nature and dirt, the worse they felt- inside and out.

Like a bad joke, one thing became increasingly clear-

> "What do you get when you routinely douse everything inside and out with germ-killers?"
>
> "Bigger Germs"

Antibiotics were in the food they ate, the soap they washed with and the cleaner they used in their homes.

At first, the germs retreated, withered and died.

Then in an awesome display of evolution, new germs appeared- resistant to the antibiotics and sometimes actually thriving in the artificially sterile environments created by them.

Aiding and abetting this new onslaught was the tremendous mobility of society. Where in the past, it took weeks, months, and even years to travel from one place to another, now it was a matter of hours- days at the most.

Germs traveled lightly, silently, inside mucous membranes, under fingernails, stuck to the bottoms of shoes.

No one alive could remember, but the history books were full of stories- telling of entire populations being decimated not by force, or physical encroachment, but by the very basic lack of natural immunities to germs not local to their area.

Explorers arrived bearing gifts and weapons, and sneezed out the real menace without even knowing it.

History has a way of repeating itself, and though the modern-day explorers wore crumpled business suits and arrived on the red-eye flight, they sneezed out the menace all the same.

Every flu season brought different strains cascading down on people from each and every nasal expulsion. The scientists scrambled and gambled to try to ensure adequate amounts of effective vaccinations.

Most people were exposed to these germs and either didn't get sick at all, or suffered through mild cases. The very young, the very old, and the constitutionally fragile were occasionally struck down and their numbers were tallied and relayed on the nightly news along with the sports scores.

The bothersome flu this season was the swine flu, and it was bothersome not only because it was the flu, but because it had the unusually bad form to be able to actually cross species- from pigs to humans, which made it particularly tricky to pin down and halt the spread of disease.

So the humans redoubled their efforts to avoid and eradicate germs- they carried anti-bacterial lotions with them, despite the fact that flu are viruses, not bacteria.

Students and workers alike were told to stay at home if they had any symptoms of illness. When there were too many students or workers missing from one spot, the rest were told to stay at home too, and the places that they went to every day were cleaned, fumigated, bleached and re-bleached.

The yearly flus were obvious, easy to track and tally, very visible and dramatic of nature. Good for the scientists, good for the news people, not generally all that bad for the population at large.

They also took peoples' minds off of the real threats and dangers- diseases of culture, diet and environment ran rampant through society, becoming so common that they were mistaken as normal.

Everyone had a family member, or several, with cancer, heart disease, diabetes, sometimes combinations or all of the three. Not only ailments of the elderly anymore, people of middle age increasingly were struck down by tumors, heart attacks, diabetic shock.

Children, too, were not immune. Kept inside most of the time to avoid the dirt and pollution of Nature, and the dangers of strangers, breathing conditioned air and playing computer games instead of running wild outdoors, they ate single serve pre-packaged foods alone watching TV.

Babies were born already packed full of hormones and antibiotics via their umbilical cord.

Making her rounds at night, she stopped at each bedside- telling stories about her childhood and giving little gifts of interesting pebbles or colorful feathers from the park, chasing their fears and cradling their dreams.

And the children drifted off to sleep with her stories echoing in their slumber- of a wondrous time filled with sunshine, and where getting dirty was not only tolerated, but required.

Where they ate food right out of the garden…without washing it first.

Chapter Thirteen

Community

Something was happening to the town.

For well over one hundred years, the town square had been the center, the heart of the community. The original homesteaders- the ones the park was named for and who left the vestiges of their habitation behind- had gifted the town's first businessmen with lots to build their stores on that surrounded the stately city hall. That somber edifice had also been built on donated land and commissioned by the first town council.

Every morning brought coffee drinkers, grocery shoppers, and bank patrons, every afternoon saw elderly domino players and children buying after-school treats. Every evening the sound of music from the corner tavern vied for attention with the brightly lit marquee of the movie theater.

Sunday mornings the square was aflutter with families in their Sunday Best on their way to or from the church with its steeple pointing the way to Everlasting Life- the only man-made structure taller than the roof of city hall.

The town square was where deals were made, romances were nurtured, and all news good or bad shared and passed on- sometimes whispered, sometimes shouted.

The town changed, people became more mobile, and the original stores gave way to new businesses that catered to a new era. There were fewer groceries and more antiques, the tavern gave way to a trendy café, and the quaint old movie theater with its balcony and carvings and velvet draperies became another church- a different church to accommodate new townspeople with different beliefs.

People still gathered there- window shopping or eating lunch or worshipping, gravitating to the park off to one side of the square- buffering the city from the fields and forests beyond.

But something was happening. Bit by bit, house by house, as families grew up and the children moved to college and then out into the bigger world that called to them with a Siren Song of adventure and riches, of things different and therefore better than what they grew up with, the houses grew quiet with emptiness.

Finally the only people who lived in town were elderly, and one by one they left their homes under their own power or not- moving to retirement homes, or the silent graveyard, or a condominium in Palm Beach.

The young people who did move back to the area moved into the new subdivisions outside of town- cookie cutter houses that morphed off of the pages of the Trendy Living magazines and sprouted up in the bulldozed fields and flattened forests like warts.

Their parents' homes had been originals, each home a public display and celebration of the personalities within.

The Mark of the Subdivision was conformity- every house was defiantly the same as the next one save perhaps the color of the front door. There was some sort of perverse comfort knowing that the interiors of your neighbors' houses were essentially the same as yours- as if stability and permanence could be so duplicated and reinforced.

Once the people with the most money to spend moved out of town, the businesses followed.

Not exactly "followed", since the merchants on the town square didn't move out, but in a manufactured example of co-dependant symbiosis, the chain stores circled the subdivisions like so many chuck wagons.

While the town square was unique to itself, a testament to the history and development of the town, the strip malls surrounding the new subdivisions echoed their strict conformity.

Anchored by big box stores, flanked by a pre-determined assortment of restaurants and specialty shops, the people flocked to the new places to shop as though they were being offered something special, instead of admitting that they could get the same food and the same items at the exact same stores built in the exact same order literally anywhere in the country- a road trip along any interstate highway coast to coast and border to border confirmed that.

It was that link, that unconscious yet very real belief that by shopping a certain way and eating at certain places "like everyone else" they would safeguard the image of the life they wanted to believe was real, and important, and true.

In a uniquely American way, an entire generation and its offspring reached to the twinkling unreachable stars of consumerism for stability instead of strengthening its already established roots of history and identity.

Even the graceful old urban churches sat empty- great fund drives had allowed the congregations to build not just new church buildings, but entire "worship complexes" outside of town- buildings, senior centers and their own schools- havens for Believers away from the very commercialism their parishioners had worked so hard to become part of.

Town squares all over the land faltered, the life sucked away from them, and all that remained were the discarded shells of society.

The park grew quieter than ever- with the eateries moved out to the strip malls and the children overwhelmingly living in the subdivisions with their brand new rigidly scheduled Fitness Centers, and the shopping being done at the chain stores, no one had any reason to walk across the street and linger awhile in the park named for the first settlers in the area.

She had the entire place to herself now, and she was grateful for the company of Daisy. They wandered in the sunshine each afternoon, enjoying the song of the birds and the antics of the squirrels, but hearing the echoes of playing children every time the breeze set the squeaky old swings in motion.

Chapter Fourteen

Faith

Danger was in the air.

It was a time to be careful, guard the children and other loved ones, and be ever vigilant.

They were unwillingly basking in a climate of Fear, and it was being nurtured by the very things that were in place to help people feel secure- the Government and the Church.

The lines were becoming blurred- those important lines that had been indelible for many years- to separate Church and State- ensuring freedom of religion for every American.

Oh, people had always voted their Faith, and that in itself wasn't a bad thing. One's Faith defines self, beliefs, morals, and rules to live by and live for.

What was new was the overt manner that God- the Christian God who was defined as a rigid and intolerant taskmaster, had been brought into the Halls of Lawmaking and Politics had started to be preached from the Pulpits of all Faiths- either in favor of this new turn of events, or against it.

The people became suspicious, watchful, divided and slowly but surely the United States became torn asunder seemingly willfully by the institutions meant to keep them united.

It was convenient for the People in Power for this to happen since folks who are busy watching their average normal neighbors for signs of terroristic activities generally have no time or inclination to observe the same behavior from those at the Top.

    And the people prayed.

They prayed for safety and they prayed for peace and they prayed for their families and they prayed for their neighbors and they prayed for the religious leaders and they prayed for the politicians and they prayed for the doctors who cared for them.

    And the people were preyed upon.

But not by nameless foreign terrorists or their neighbors who they watched ever so closely,

But by the Government who made laws that stripped them of the very freedoms it claimed to be protecting.

By the religious leaders who preached suspicion and hatred despite reading from a book that espoused Judging Not Lest Ye Be Judged,

And by the very doctors and scientists whose income depended not on how many people remained well, but by how many people they were able to medicate, mechanically look inside of, eventually cut open, and repeat.

The Government sent children- their own and their neighbors'- off to war- a war to secure freedom in faraway lands. But it was really a war to secure the oil the country was so addicted to.

And the religious leaders praised the righteousness of war and the sacrifices of their children in the fight for freedom and against terrorism, and made sure to re-enforce fear of entire populations whose god was just as rigid and intolerant as their own, only in a bad way.

And the doctors put the pieces of children who came back home together again

> But they were never the same.

And no one questioned out loud how it was patriotic for our government to spend billions of dollars on war and death overseas, but treasonous to ask it to spend anything that guaranteed health and life for its own people at home.

Religion spread into the news media- that bastion of "fair and unbiased coverage" became one more sounding board for both sides- those that wanted to "Bring God back into the government" and simultaneously those who fought not for freedom OF religion, but freedom FROM religion.

Both camps decried the other for being the very Instrument of Destruction of the Nation, which was, there was no doubt about it, very surely being destroyed.

Ironically, while the religious leaders and the politicians called on the people to beware of the Holy War- the Jihad, that would rain down doom on everything and everyone held precious from far off places at the hands of shifty-eyed foreigners, the soul of the land was being poisoned from within- and it spewed from the hearts and the mouths of those self-same leaders.

The people trusted the leaders…at first.

By and by, the hearts of the politicians showed to be untrue and untrustworthy, and the people turned to the religious leaders.

Being only humans, after all, the religious leaders proved to be just as susceptible to the Intoxication of Power, and the corruption ate through the foundations of organized religion.

Orphaned by the mortal mouthpieces of both God the Father and the Government of the Motherland, the people drifted without direction or purpose- realizing for the first time in their lives that they themselves were not important to anyone in either Institution-

They'd been raised in a society that taught them everyone was special, everyone had potential, and everyone mattered.

And now, they saw very clearly that they didn't.

By and by, elections were held and no one showed up- it didn't matter who they voted for- the big corporations owned them all.

By and by, the churches closed their doors- people who believed in the Intolerant and Fearsome God had become furtive and private, believing that to survive, they needed to care for none but their own, and were increasingly suspicious of anyone.

People who believed in the Tolerant God of Love and Renewal kept to themselves and hoped for the best, but feared the wild eyes of their former friends who called for things like Justice and Security, while doling out their own brand of vigilantism- out in the open from the empty pulpits or the news anchor chairs or the floor of Congress or the Senate, and by cover of darkness- if they felt it was for the Good of the Country.

Years of waste- wasting water and food and natural resources, wasting money and time because they were ever so plentiful, having traveled fast and far and without care, the people had been too busy being prosperous to stop, to listen to the very real warnings that had been right in front of them.

Suddenly they were poor and jobless and homeless and had no idea how it had happened.

Their food and water and energy supplies were exhausted and they were incredulous- there had been so much, for so long.

They were a people living in a country that was economically and socially bankrupt and they'd been so focused on being alert to the dangers outside of their borders that they never even saw it coming, even though it took a long time to get there.

> The greatest nation in the world was on its knees,
> And not a shot had been fired.

Looking forward to the yearly pageant, she read the notice on the church door with disappointment, but not surprise-

Christmas program cancelled

Due to lack of funds and interest

Our apologies to the children

God Bless America

Please

Part Three

2012

"Amazingly Resilient"

Chapter Fifteen

Water

The Children's Hospital grew larger from need, the children being the quickest to fall from societal illnesses- heart disease, diabetes, cancer, obesity and the accompanying complications of those maladies of prosperity- and along with the businesses and churches, the hospital migrated right out of town and onto a monstrous, sprawling, carnivorous medical complex.

The abandoned hospital was turned into a large shelter-slash-clinic for the homeless, the old one having long been too small to embrace the throngs of needy that grew every day.

By night the subdivisions would shed the jobless and foreclosed-upon silently, cloaked with the shame of circumstance and they'd appear the next day at the shelters looking proud, resentful, confused and grieved all at the same time.

So although the tiny patients she'd tended to were gone, there was still plenty for her to do, for she found new focus in consoling the children whose parents were physically there, but mentally far far away either from the shell shock of being stripped of their lifestyles, or lost to chemical dependency (generally brought on by the shell shock).

During the day these children were in school or daycare, but at night when everyone's demons were the strongest, they were alone in the dark- their parents were clinging to their own sanity precariously enough and had no energy left for their offspring.

So she gathered them to her at night- some clutching teddy bears or blankets and some bereft of anything familiar- and she tucked them around each other and told stories from her heart- fragmented pieces of the thousands of library books she'd read to the children at the hospital, shuffled up and re-cast.

Some were filled with adventure, some with wondrous fairy tale creatures, some with gentle everyday characters, but they all ended the same way.

"And they all lived happily ever after".

And she gave them a drink, and she kissed their foreheads, and she stroked their cheeks, and they drifted off to sleep with the last thing on their mind not how hungry they were, or how scared they were or how much they missed their 'old' mommies and daddies, but dreaming and believing in Happily Ever After.

She ate freely and for free at the shelter trough again, and though she did not officially belong there, never once was she questioned. She had never lost the 'look of the homeless', and she fit in seamlessly, silently, invisibly.

In the mornings she still worked at the thrift store three days a week- that had not moved out of town, but remained staunchly where it was- although the people shopping there were more and more the ones who had previously donated their discards.

They weeded through the clothing and the toys, and more than a few of them remembered with a twinge of shame tossing items in a black trash sack that were very stained, or mightily torn, or obviously broken beyond repair and thinking at the time, "Well, they're poor- they'll be grateful for what they get".

And now, in their new life, when they found something usable, they were grateful for what they got.

By afternoon, she was all too ready to go home to her sunny little room in the now completely deserted park- the gates had been locked against trespassers, vagrants and vandals but she was slight and slipped easily through a gap in the fence on the backside of the property.

There were trespassers, vagrants and vandals to be sure- unemployed young men and women who roamed without purpose and with frustration, but there was nothing in the park of value to them, and along with herself, the park became completely invisible.

She and Daisy walked out of sight of the town square, and she breathed fresh air and listened to the birds, and looked on with worry as the one pond that was left turned a sickly green and then disappeared.

It worried her because while the park pond was turning green, the sips of water she passed around to the children at bedtime had ceased coming from the faucet- the drinking water for the shelter was being trucked in and distributed by the bottle.

The official line was that the city water was not drinkable 'temporarily', but it had been months and there was no sign of ever being able to drink from the faucets again.

Laundry washing was strictly monitored, and even showers were limited due to the water shortage.

The huge aquifers had finally been taxed to their capacity, and, while not empty, were coughing up all the things that had dropped to their bottoms over the centuries of filtration, and it was not good.

The rains still came, and the snow still fell, so the aquifers were recharging, but not quickly enough to keep society going as they were used to.

Water had always been plentiful and they'd taken it for granted, and they were used to getting it from the aquifers at the turn of a faucet and they were oblivious to any other way to get it.

In her garden, she was careful to gather as much rainwater as she could- she placed buckets at the ends of the old metal rainspouts that were still on the barn. These she lined up, covered, till she needed them to water her plants.

Her little hand pump was still happily producing good, clean water, and she hummed along with the squeak of the pump handle, filling her teapot to heat her afternoon cocoa- taking just enough for one cup of cocoa, and enough left over to wash the cup.

She was so used to being alone, she almost dropped the teapot when she heard a small voice ask shyly, "What are you doing"? Crouched among the weeds and flowers and flowering weeds was a little girl she recognized from the shelter- just ten hours ago she'd tucked her under the covers. The little girl had sleep in her eyes and tousled hair the same color as the doll she clutched protectively.

A little alarmed that she'd been followed, a little angry with herself for not being aware, she was nonetheless most concerned with how the girl looked- very pale, very thin, and very frightened. Barefoot, too small for the faded sundress, the girl was painfully the least vibrant blossom in the garden.

She held out her hand and the girl smiled quickly and scurried to her, and Daisy woofed quietly once, then swished her tail and waggled her eyebrows in welcome.

She explained to the girl how the pump worked, and pumped just enough more water for a second cup of cocoa.

Just as quickly as she'd smiled, the girl scowled and turned away.

"My dad says there ain't no more clean water- says that's why we have to buy it and be careful with it. The only water I'm supposed to drink is the water in the bottles".

She clucked sadly and said to Daisy, "Well, Daisy- I guess our new friend won't be wanting any cocoa- would you like her share?"

And they spent the rest of the afternoon drinking cocoa, and she explained to her new friend Emily how the pump works, and about the underground stream that fed it and why she saved rainwater to give to her plants between the times it really rained and how precious water is and the never ending magical cleansing cycle of precipitation, evaporation, and filtration that looks to those not familiar with magic like rain, and puddles, and mud.

They walked back to the shelter in time for dinner, and Emily wrinkled her nose when she drank the artificially tasteless bottled water, because she now knew water- real water- and how it tasted full of trace minerals and the earth that cleansed it, and the seeds of that knowledge sprouted and took root in a mind not warped by care or corroded by money or crazy with despair.

Chapter Sixteen

Food

The farmers market that had flourished in the town square every Saturday during the brief Good Food Revival had dwindled, but like the hardy varieties of vegetables sold there, had not died out.

She spent every night at the shelter, and although she loved the children and was aware of how important she was to them, the pressing depression that permeated the place wore her down and she needed to find a calming, renewing source of interaction to recharge her spirit for the long hours filled with darkness of every kind.

One day, crossing through the town square on her way home, she heard someone say, "Good morning".

Never slowing her pace, since she was sure it was directed at someone else, she stopped in her tracks when it was repeated- louder but not unkindly. "Good morning, ma'am. That's a lovely purple hat. Would you like an apple? One of the very last of last year's crop".

She turned around and met the gaze of the speaker- a woman about her age wearing a denim work shirt tucked into a flowing flowered skirt. Scuffed and worn work boots peeked out from underneath the skirt and doing its best to contain unruly volumes of graying auburn hair was unbelievably the twin of her own purple hat.

The woman laughed and her brown eyes sparkled. "You have most excellent taste in headgear", she said, and the other farmers chuckled and nodded.

Thoughtfully chewing the apple on her way home she pondered on both the amazing crispness and flavor of the apple and the odd fact that the entire group of adults had actually seen her.

She started spending her Saturday mornings visiting with the farmers- some older folks like herself and Sofia- the woman who'd first spoken to her- gnarled hands and weathered features only accentuating the sparkle in their eyes and the honesty of their smiles, along with the 'new' younger farmers- those either born into it or those who'd been born with the drive to learn, to live, the hard life of a farmer and who knowingly exchanged the 9 to 5 and the 401K for the 24/7 and the security of knowing that they could feed- really feed- their families no matter the size of their bank account.

After a few weeks she got up the nerve to ask Sofia what was most confusing to her- during a quiet break in the morning, she said, "You know, for years I've been quite invisible to everyone but children and dogs. A few adults here and there have seen me but generally not unless I call attention to myself. Yet everyone here saw me clearly and at once. I wonder why that is?"

Sofa smiled kindly and answered without pause. "We're farmers, dear. We tend to ignore things that really don't matter and pay special attention to things that do". And she offered her a slice of fresh baked bread slathered with raspberry jam.

They talked about her work at the shelter and the children.

They talked about her work at the thrift store.

They talked about Sofia's farm and family- the loss of her husband to death and her children to spouses, and jobs and busyness.

To have a friend to talk to- a woman her own age- was something she hadn't had in a long time. Of course there was no way of knowing just how long it had been, but it felt very good to have it back.

She carefully told snippets and bits about her home- mostly about the little garden spot, and Daisy. Sofia never pried or asked for any more information than was freely given and she considered that the mark of a true friendship- respect.

They exchanged garden gifts- she brought hollyhock seeds and peony corms from around the old house foundation- varieties that were difficult to find anymore- and Sofia brought her seedlings and seeds for many kinds of heirloom vegetables, which were planted with honor here and there among the others.

Every time Sofia brought her something to plant, she made sure to write down very specific directions for care on whatever paper she could find in her pockets- old napkins, envelopes, the backs of receipts.

One morning Sofia did not bring her something to plant. Instead she handed her a small blank journal for her to gather up and organize her garden notes. "I'd love to see your garden sometime", Sofia said gently.

Leery of anyone getting too close to her home, but trusting Sofia she said, "Of course- how rude of me. It's not really in my yard- there's too much shade there- just in a sunny place I found near my house."

After the farmers market closed down for the day, she helped Sofia clean up her spot, and they walked to the backside of the park fence- both easily squeezing through the gap.

Through the deserted park grown wild and cheery with neglect, Sofia gasped with delight as they rounded the tall unmanicured shrubberies and were suddenly in the middle of her garden, flowers and vegetables tucked here and there in stern disregard for rhyme or reason.

"How lovely!" Sofia breathed, and dropped to her knees to better appreciate the patchwork of weeds and domesticated flowers before her.

Puzzled, Sofia turned to her. "Where do you live? To be this beautiful, you must be watering your plants somehow- they look so lush- surely you're not carrying water here?"

Shyly smiling, she carefully parted the screen of foliage that surrounded the pump.

The treasure of having water in town that was not polluted nor regulated was not lost on Sofia.

They had discussed at length the concern they both had for all those at the shelter, but especially the children, who were fed nothing but canned vegetables and fruits. Sofia had met Emily several times and had heard about the nights at the shelter doing volunteer work that kept young hearts secure and young minds able to sleep unafraid of the dark.

To bring fresh, good food to these people would be a worthy cause all the market farmers agreed, but all were big of heart and short on cash, and there seemed to be no way to do it

Unless

A place could be found that was near the shelter and could be used free of charge to plant a garden so designated- all it would take were the 'extras'- extra seedlings, extra tools, extra seeds and a small amount of time commitment from each market farmer.

One of the farmers had read about a movement overseas- stealth planting of edible food where there would normally be lawn grass, or weeds, or trash.

It was called Guerilla Gardening, and it appealed to their collective hearts.

Under cover of night, the hole in the fence was made just large enough to allow a tiller to be pushed through it before springing back into place protectively.

The park itself seemed intent on keeping their secret.

At the shelter, first lettuces appeared. Not anemic tasteless iceberg lettuce rusting as they ate it, but fresh, spicy leaves that were every shade of green and lovely maroons and pinks- tossed into salads so delightful it seemed wrong to douse them with bottled dressing.

She went to the kitchen armed with a handful of bulbs and suggested a simple dressing to the workers- olive oil, cider vinegar and crushed garlic- shaken and tossed into the leaves making them even more vibrant and glistening with life.

The lettuces were followed by beans in colors and shapes as extraordinary as the lettuces, and every few weeks brought new fruits and vegetables- eaten either raw or cooked ever so briefly and none of them doused in sauces or salt.

Children and adults alike were enchanted by the variety and the flavors of things they'd grown up thinking of as 'barely tolerable and almost inedible but good for you'.

Mealtimes became more than a mile marker in the trudging journey of their days- they were anticipated, mysterious, celebratory.

That food- good food, not those sweets and fats generally considered 'comfort food'- should be anything more than fuel for the body was a new concept for a lot of them, including the employees and shelter volunteers.

The note attached to the boxes of produce read simply

> To your health and happiness
> From your friends at the farmers market

And business at the farmers market grew once again as word spread from the shelter staff, to their families and friends and beyond.

The rising price of gasoline had rendered 'fresh' fruits and veggies at the big box stores scarce and expensive, and the argument against unsanitary local foods was overridden by the luscious fact that the farmers market produce was not only more tasty, it was now cheaper than the sanitized wax orbs in the produce aisle.

Only Emily knew exactly where the new menu items came from, and she smiled just a little wider than the others at the tables- the tables that had become transformed from gloomy feeding troughs into true dining tables where they shared meals, thoughts, ideas and even hope.

Chapter Seventeen

Shelter

Just as quickly as they'd sprung up, garish glamorous slashes on the landscape, the subdivisions withered and faded from the lack of gasoline to nourish and sustain them.

The people who were lucky enough to still have their jobs to commute to started carpooling, which worked for a while.

As jobs disappeared folks started looking for local employment, which worked for a while.

Eventually, the houses in the subdivisions that were occupied became a minority as folks moved away, moved back in with relatives to save expenses, walked away from their lifestyles and their self-images and were sucked down what seemed to most of them to be a giant backwards hole of regression.

The lucky ones had family to move in with or were able to secure local employment and were able to rent little houses in town- the very ones they'd escaped from on their upwardly mobile flight into the blinding sun of the subdivisions.

They shopped in the farmers market because it was something they could do without driving, and it was cheaper than the store prices, and the farmers were generous with suggestions and seedlings and seeds for things the people could grow themselves in their sunny little yards behind their quaint little houses.

Vegetable gardens appeared where once there had been nothing but sterile manicured lawns, and most garages were given partially over to a few rabbit hutches, or a hen house, or even a dairy goat peeking out of a doghouse, smugly.

It was a period of urban renewal, but in the beginning those in the middle of it felt anything but renewed. They did what they did out of necessity, not because they wanted to.

After a while, though, they realized that what they were doing now was so much more than they'd been doing before- before they were going to work to make money to go to the store to buy food. Now they were feeding their families.

And the police officers and the city council members looked the other way over code violations regarding livestock within city limits- since most of them had become part of the urban renewal as well.

The others- and there were many more others than anyone wanted to admit to- drifted here and there, the children delivered to school every day while their parents picked up cash jobs as they could, eating in the shelter or church kitchens, and sleeping in their cars if they still had cars. If not, they found odd places that afforded some semblance of a roof from the rain and walls from the wind.

Quite a few of them ended up in the park at night.

Of course they were not supposed to be there, but honestly, it was argued at the city council meetings, where else could they go?

And they told the police officers to look the other way as long as the people were orderly and quiet.

So the lines for hot meals were long and wound around the shelter building, and those in line were fed in shifts and the volunteers and shelter workers and police officers and city council members tried not to think about just how many people were 'out there' the rest of the time.

There were several group pavilions in the park- built for parties and reunions and whatnot- and these filled up at night with the shelter overflow.

Families and single people, senior citizens and children, all shared the same look of puzzled fuzziness- they were unsure of how they had gotten from normalcy to sleeping on a hard bench in a park pavilion.

Their entire existence had taken on such a surreal feel that it was not surprising to any of them that every night there was a new pile of offerings to be divided amongst themselves- blankets, pillows, coats, hats, socks, toiletries, flashlights, books and magazines.

So the items were divvied up, and the pavilions started looking, if not like their old houses, at least more like home.

One day there was a different sort of pile- seeds, seedlings, garden tools and directions written in small precise letters. The next morning, those who didn't have work or school to attend to were planting their garden because any roots are better than no roots at all.

And she worked sorting other people's discarded clothing in the morning, took her pay in things to make other people comfortable in their new and unwanted lives, spent her nights comforting other people's children and spent her afternoons in her garden with Daisy and in their room drinking tea and napping.

She worried about all the people who were homeless.

But she did what she could to help them.

Chapter Eighteen

Security

Nights had become problematic.

The children started out in their respective spots, fanning out from her calm presence- little spokes of life wrapped in fuzzy blankets and clutching stuffed animals and dolls.

With every outburst in the dark, the blankets inched closer to her and by morning she was suffocating in a living cocoon of swaddled youngsters pressing in on her.

The shattered nights had come with the broken young man.

Dressed head to toe in camo gear, he'd appeared one morning and as a single person and a veteran, had been allowed to stay.

During the day he perched rather than sat, and was never completely still, quiet but on edge, hypersensitive to everything and everyone around him.

He talked softly and quickly to himself in a running never-ending dialogue, constantly furtively casting sidelong glances in every direction and repetitively patting at his side, checking for a weapon that wasn't there anymore.

Not surprisingly, he sat alone at the dinner table.

She asked the shelter social worker where he'd come from and what was known about him.

His name was Mike and he'd come home from war physically intact but mentally vaporized.

Not recognizing who their son had become, and feeding off of the alien fear that flashed from his eyes, the atmosphere in their home had gone from joyful homecoming to dismayed confusion when he didn't bounce back into his former life but sank deeper and deeper into the nightmares in his mind. The images that were plastered onto the backs of his retinas and never ever went away tangled up with the echoes of war and the reek of violence and it became all too clear that although he was home, he'd never be there again.

The nights were the worst- without the careful waking attention to keep the demons at bay they exploded into life as soon as he slept, and he screamed and swore and beseeched a god who never listened to make it stop.

To just make it stop.

So they'd had him hospitalized, and drugged, and kissed him goodbye and went home to mourn him as if he were dead.

When he'd had all the treatment and care that was allowed for such things, and had been sufficiently subdued by the medications, he was asked if he wanted to call his family to come get him.

He told them calmly, "No thank you, Sir- no need to trouble them. I know the way home".

When he shuffled into the shelter six months later, hungry and dirty, un-medicated and twitchy, the social worker found his ID in his wallet and was able to track down his family, who'd fallen on their own hard times, wished him the best, declared their love for him, but declined to come get him.

"I've called the hospital and they can't take him back. I'm afraid if he keeps disrupting everyone's sleep, I'll have to call the police to come get him for disorderly conduct. I hate it but don't know what else to do", the social worker told her.

"Let me try something. Give me a week", she asked, and the tranquility of her gaze had the social worker nodding approval before even realizing it.

She started by sitting at the very opposite end of the table as Mike during meal times. Never taking her eyes off of her plate, she talked to herself quietly and calmly- at the same volume as Mike's steady chatter- not to override him, but just loud enough to be sure to be heard.

The first day she talked of the weather- the color of the sky, the smell of the air.

And he seemed to ignore her.

The second day she talked of the food they were eating- what it was, where it came from, why it was good.

And there were tiny imperceptible gaps in Mike's mumblings.

The third day she told the exact same story she had told the children the night before.

And he fell silent with listening.

The fourth day she looked directly at him while telling the story, prepared for him to bolt and run.

He didn't. He locked onto her face unblinkingly- steadying himself, pulling himself as if by force into the security of her eyes.

The fifth day she told him that she'd been hospitalized, or that's what she'd been told. Hospitalized for not being able to recall anything or anyone from a certain time period- she could relay things that happened while she was a child. She could

remember her way home today, and her day-to-day routines. But huge chunks of her adult life were missing and she didn't know why or how. It was her curse that she lived with every day-
        She couldn't remember.
Tears formed at the corners of Mike's eyes and he uttered the first words that weren't angry mutterings or agonized screams-
        "I can't forget".

Daisy liked children and women, but had a distrust of men. When the door to the room opened and Mike entered first, she startled awake and woofed in alarm. She calmed quickly when she saw her friend, and quizzically looked from her to Mike- other than Emily no one had been in their room- even Sofia.

The shadow of a smile flickered at the edges of Mike's mouth.

"I had a dog when I was a kid. He was the best friend I ever had".

And Daisy's tail swish swish swished in approval and her eyebrows waggled in acceptance.

Mike's smile evaporated while they were drinking their cocoa. "You mean you live here all alone- aren't you afraid? There are a lot of bad people out there".

She chuckled and told him how handy it was to have nothing anyone wanted- to possess nothing but invisibility.

Nevertheless, Mike had been trained, and trained well, to assume the worst and take a defensive stance in all situations.

He believed with all his heart that he moved from the shelter into the loft in the barn to watch out for her- an old frail lady with an old frail dog alone and defenseless in the world.

During the day he read endlessly from the books she brought him- everything from humor to philosophy to history were devoured by his mind that'd been starved by horror and senseless destruction.

The shelter was once again quiet and peaceful at night and the children slept well.

And there were no cries from the loft- Mike slept soundly and unmolested by demons at his new post- protecting the person who had brought him gently to safety.

Chapter Nineteen

Health

The flu season was particularly harrowing that year.

Not that this strain of germs was any more deadly than those in previous years, but that the people were ill-equipped to deal with it in what they had come to assume was the usual and preferred manner.

The surge of unemployment meant more than loss of lifestyle, loss of income, loss of homes and cars- it meant the loss of health insurance.

Those who could afford the 'after dis-employment' premiums still found themselves without coverage if they remained unemployed after the 6 months it was in effect for, and in the current economy there was an almost 100% chance of remaining unemployed.

Without health insurance, any visit to the doctor was carefully weighed for merit and importance- Pay As You go medical care ranges from costly to wildly out of reach.

"Well visits" became a thing of the past, as preventive medicine was considered frivolous and wasteful, and hospitalizations were a rarity unless the patient was at death's door- not a good starting point for a speedy recovery.

Those who had been able to maintain their lifestyles went to the doctor for medicines and sometimes were hospitalized to stave off dehydration, and generally felt run down and run over for weeks after the initial infection.

People who lived in shelters and who ate regular shelter fare, along with children eating school lunches and old folks in retirement homes fared the worst- the experts assumed that it was the close contact day in and day out and stressed the wearing of masks and the usage of anti-bacterial wash and generally the separation of humans from one another.

Unaccountably, the folks at the local shelter were not getting nearly as sick as those in other shelters nationwide.

Many things were examined and discussed- from the ethnic backgrounds of this particular shelter, to the local climate, to the soaps used to wash dishes and clothing and floors and children, and all those hypotheses were hashed over at the dinner table- fresh veggies piled high on their plates.

The folks who were supplementing their diets with backyard-grown produce were also staying healthier, as well as, amazingly, the families living in the park.

Sleeping in the fresh air instead of the re-breathed atmosphere of the shelter went a long way to stopping the spread of germs.

And with the loss of health insurance, people were not able to afford any number of drugs they'd been on- cholesterol, blood pressure, diabetes and even some heart medications had to be eliminated- some of them cost upwards of several hundred dollars a month, and who had that kind of money?

Trips to the grocery store were less frequent, and items were bought in bulk that could be used several different ways. Flour and sugar were purchased instead of boxed cake mixes, plain pasta and blocks of cheese replaced packages of noodles and powdered cheese product.

Menus became simple and fresh and without all the added colorings and preservatives eating became cheaper, healthier and more satisfying.

In spite of their stress from being unemployed, blood pressure went down.

In spite of their heartache at losing everything they'd worked for, heart disease became less common.

People who were dead set on maintaining their old diets of highly processed foods remained in their state of ill health.

People who turned to alcohol or drugs to cope with their problems developed all the illnesses associated with those addictions.

But by and large, changing from a highly processed expensive lifestyle to a simple and more frugal one had resulted in healthier people who didn't worry quite so much anymore about their lack of "health care".

That was the year she got the flu.

Normally very hale, she continued going to work and tending her children and her garden until she just felt too bad and stayed in bed, aching from her hair to her toenails.

Mike knocked on the door, and peeked in on her- worry washing over his face.

"It's nothing, dear- I'll be fine in a few days."

And he fed her soup, and cocoa, and fresh tidbits from the garden, and helped her outside to sit in the sunshine every day, and tucked her in at night.

Emily brought her flowers and told her stories, and Sofia gave Mike herbal teas to give her.

It was more than a few days, but it really wasn't very long before she and Daisy were out and about again- because they had things to do, places to be, and people to take care of.

Chapter Twenty

Community

It had seemed like forever, but it was really just the blink of the cosmic eye- the high wild ride provided by technology fueled by oil-fueled technology.

It's a survival instinct to assume that the way things are today are they way they will always be- that assumption protects an organism from focusing on things other than day to day living- finding food, water, shelter.

In the world of animals, if something changes, that new reality becomes true as though it has always been. An animal that loses a limb and manages to heal will not mourn the loss- it will just adjust, adapt, and carry on. Time in an arbitrary way has no meaning- leave the house to go to work, realize you've forgotten your lunch and go back within ten minutes. You'll be met at the door by your dog with as much fervor as if you'd been gone all day.

Humans have the dubious distinction of being able to reside in the present, wallow in the past and reach for the future simultaneously.

During the downward slide of Life as They Knew It, everyone had had twinges of un-ease, even if they never acknowledged them.

These feelings had displayed publicly as people who were more religious or less religious, more socially-minded or more clannish, more to the extreme left of the political spectrum or leaning way to the right, folks who hoarded food and toilet paper and gold and guns or folks who spent every penny earned or borrowed on things that would prove and ensure their worth and security.

Society as a whole was looking for the Big Event- that one thing that would spell the end of an era- something huge, dramatic, cataclysmic- something that could be pointed at forever after as

The Moment that Changed Everything

And there were moments like that for sure just as there have always been- wars and explosions and natural disasters crashing down and around and through, but even all those things together did not cause the shift in how they lived.

She'd seen it and recognized it for what it was.

What they were doing- just because they could- was living life too large, too fast, too busy and so intent on focusing on the Big Picture that they didn't realize what tiny specks on the canvas

They themselves really were

And how very precious were the tiny specks around them.

So she watched, helpless and invisible, as society did not blow up in a blaze of glory, but crumbled quietly- one tiny ember at a time.

One by one the families fell- by unemployment, or foreclosure, or divorce, or illness. A surprising number fell from over-abundance- emotionally separated from each other by possessions and occupations.

When faced with changes not of their own making, they reacted in un-natural yet predictable manners.

Peaceful people turned surly and occasionally violent.

People who had been regarded as poor reached out to help those new to the class.

There were some riots fueled by anger and frustration- but they burned fast, furious and then dissipated, and some groups who'd already been closing in on themselves found false security in further isolation- where they generally encountered social suffocation caused by the tightly packed aura of suspicion and mistrust.

By and large, most of the people in most of the places had less money, adjusted to less prestigious employment options and living arrangements, shifted the way they lived, re-grouped and moved on.

And although every person and every family and every group fought their new reality and mourned the things they'd lost, and felt acutely that no one had encountered such injustice or sorrow, what they were going through was simply evolution- whether or not they believed in it.

She'd seen it from a distance and up close- watched those around her push and soar and reach for the sky, eyes and hearts willing themselves to defy gravity.

And she quietly tended the garden and the dog and the children and patiently waited for the gentle yet unavoidable backswing.

She really didn't have any other options, and she had plenty of time.

To the casual traveler on an interstate highway, the miles and miles of empty strip malls and abandoned subdivisions spoke of failure and poverty.

To an old woman and her dog sitting in the sunshine on a park bench, watching, listening, smelling the town square shake itself back to life after a long hibernation of neglect, seeing children playing in the fountain like little rainbow fishes because now their families were too poor for any other entertainment

    It was absolutely fabulous.

Chapter Twenty One

Faith

And life went on, the way it generally does- things always seem to work out- not usually the way you expect them to or want them to, but they work out all the same.

At least that's what she believed, - not from memory or hyperbole, but from what she lived every day.

They were sitting in the sunshine, as they liked to do- she and Daisy and Emily- after working in the garden one afternoon.

There hadn't been much to do with the growing season coming to an end and the winter shadows setting in early, but the breeze was still warm and cozy and she dozed just a little bit- resting her eyes while Daisy kept watch and Emily tucked her big soft sweater around them both.

Quite by accident, her frayed and faded wallet fell out of her pocket and Emily picked it up- gathering the few scraps that had floated from inside it and tucking them back where they came from. She stopped mid-tuck when she got to the medical card- there was the photo of her friend much younger, but clearly still the same soft eyes and unruly hair.

Next to the photo the card read

(Smudge where the name would be)
12-21-1942
"Early Onset Dementia"

Emily gently replaced the card, kissed her on the cheek and went to find Mike.

She couldn't remember, of course, if she'd ever had a surprise party before, or any party at all for that matter, but she was surely surprised by this one.

The 21st fell on a Saturday, and she stopped at the farmers market as always on her way home from the shelter.

Market day had turned into a social event of sorts for the town, so a lot of people milling about in the town square were not anything out of the ordinary.

What was out of the ordinary was the chair offered to her in Sofia's booth, and the folks who seemed to appear out of nowhere with gifts for her- Sofia of course, and the other farmers, but also Mike and Emily and many people from the shelter, and the thrift store, and even the families from the park.

The cake was astoundingly beautiful- decorated with flowers of every shape and color and in pale lavender letters it said

Happy 70th Birthday Purple Hat Granny

"Do you like it?" asked Emily shyly, climbing up into her lap.

"I don't like it- I LOVE it!" she whispered, hugging Emily close.

Emily's eyes lost just a little of their sparkle.

"I'm sorry it doesn't have your name on it, Granny. All I could read on your card was the birthday".

"What IS your name?"

All these last invisible years, no one had asked directly what her name was until this very minute, and Emily's question pierced a flash of lightening through the cloud surrounding her memory and it let loose of one brilliant jewel from her past.

"Faith, my dear. My name is Faith".

**We are all tiny
And almost invisible**

**How we act
Towards each other
Declares our humanity**

**How we re-act
Under pressure
Defines our souls**

The characters in this story reside only in the
author's mind,
Except for Daisy
Who was my shadow for 15 years
I placed her here
For safe-keeping
The day I lost her to kidney failure.

The settings and scenarios, unfortunately
Are true
And here
And eating us alive

Now is the time
To learn
And change
And return to the Earth
For we are organic beings

Not plastic, or metal, or oil

We've been here less than a second
In Earth's timeline
Far less time than the dinosaurs
But unlike any other extinction
Ever
Ours is of our own willful doing

Sheri Dixon is an ol' treehuggin' hippiechick
Who lives in East Texas
And just does the best she knows how

Please visit her at
www.sheri-dixon.com

Made in the USA
Charleston, SC
01 December 2012